THE SEE SERIES

TYNDALE
MOMENTUM®

A Tyndale nonfiction imprint

PHILIPPIANS

A DEVOTIONAL COMMENTARY

CHRIS TIEGREEN

See your life with new eyes

Visit Tyndale online at tyndale.com.

Visit Tyndale Momentum online at tyndalemomentum.com.

Tyndale, Tyndale's quill logo, *Tyndale Momentum*, and the Tyndale Momentum logo are registered trademarks of Tyndale House Ministries. Tyndale Momentum is the nonfiction imprint of Tyndale House Publishers, Carol Stream, Illinois.

Philippians: A Devotional Commentary: See Your Life with New Eyes

Designed by Dean H. Renninger

Published in association with the literary agency of Mark Sweeney and Associates, Carol Stream, Illinois

For information about special discounts for bulk purchases, please contact Tyndale House Publishers at csresponse@tyndale.com, or call 1-855-277-9400.

ISBN 978-1-4964-8537-3

Printed in India

31 30 29 28 27 26 25
7 6 5 4 3 2 1

To Jon, Mattie, Zuri, and Arlo

Contents

The See Series

Human beings live by vision. We're directed by the images in our minds. We pursue goals when we can *see* them; we grow according to examples we've observed more than the knowledge we've learned; and we embrace hope, despair, and numerous other perspectives based on what we see happening around us. Even people who don't think of themselves as visionary tend to have some mental picture of where they are headed and why. It's the way we're wired.

Most of us have a big vision—a sense of ultimate meaning and destiny, or even just a dream or a goal for our lives. We want to live with purpose. We orient our lives by what we can picture.

We also have smaller visions—what's on the agenda for today, this week, this year, or even the next couple of decades—that shape our short-term decisions.

If our little visions and big vision don't align with each other, we feel frustrated and compromised, as if our lives are going nowhere and our desires may never be fulfilled. But if we can align these visions and see clearly, we grow steadily, even dramatically, into our purpose and calling.

SEE, BE, LIVE

Christian teaching hasn't always recognized our visionary nature. Much instruction over the years has been based on a know-it-then-do-it approach to Scripture—as if life change were simply a matter of learning the truth and then applying it. But such an approach bypasses heart transformation and can easily become legalistic and frustrating.

Though knowing and doing are both very important, following Jesus is more than a matter of knowledge and willpower. We can never *will* ourselves to be who we need to be. We are not called simply to *do*; we are called to *be*. When we put knowing and doing before being, we end up in the same condition that many of the scribes and Pharisees of Jesus' time found themselves in—as pious people aiming to live godly lives without the necessary inner transformation.

Let me explain what I mean by *knowing*—an unfortunately imprecise word in English. We might read the Bible and *know* the commandments, instructions, encouragement, and truth it conveys. We receive that information and even agree with it. And if we want to be obedient, we will act on what we know. In that sense, our approach is both cognitive and behavioral—our thoughts affect our actions. But knowledge alone won't change our hearts, motives, desires, impulses, and everything else in us that needs to be transformed.

We see this phenomenon in the multitudes of people who memorize Jesus' words about faith but still lie awake all night with worry; who love Psalm 23 but still believe they are pursued by misfortune, not goodness and mercy; who agree that Jesus is Lord but don't live as though he is. Knowledge and action alone aren't comprehensive and compelling enough to reshape us.

In addition to our intellectual or informational knowledge, we also live from a particular worldview that shapes everything about us. This, too, is *knowing*, but it's a radically different kind of knowledge, isn't it? It's how we see the world, which is why I prefer words such as *seeing* and *vision* to capture it. This kind of knowledge goes well beyond information and instructions. It reflects not only *what* we know but also *how* we know and how we *respond* (perhaps even unconsciously) to what we know. It forms our sense of identity and becomes the filter for every piece of information we receive. Whereas the first kind of knowing may shape our *thoughts* to a degree, this kind shapes our *thought processes* (and therefore our thoughts) to a greater degree.

For example, if I dive into a lake or ocean and swim around for an hour or two, I experience something of marine life. I can practice different strokes, get used to holding my breath for longer periods, and work on distances and techniques. I *know* swimming. I might even start to think I swim like a fish. But if I'm a fish, moving around in the water is my nature. I don't even have to think about strokes or breath or what it takes to live in the water. I just do it. I know swimming without even knowing that I know it. It's part of who I am.

God has given us a new nature and called us to live from it. It's a radical transformation—so radical that we aren't quite sure how to do it. Many of us turn back to old paradigms, trying to live out our new life by reforming our old nature. We try to make the new ways "natural," often by disciplining ourselves to conform to what we believe is true. In other words, we *know* and *do* by receiving information and acting on it.

But what if we really saw ourselves as new creations and gave no thought to any other possibility? What if it never even occurred to us that God might not be working in all the circumstances of our lives? What if love and worship were the default settings of our lives and we were shocked by anything else that came out of our hearts? What if our new nature was . . . well, natural?

There is no flip of a switch that gets us there, but some ways are better than others. I've experienced the futility of self-discipline born of knowing and doing (which, again, though insufficient, are still important). But I've also experienced the transformation that comes from that second kind of knowing—the radical reorientation of a worldview that shapes everything about us.

I call this radical reorientation *seeing* because we often express this deeper, more comprehensive knowledge in visual terms.

"I know you told me this would work, but I didn't *see* how."

"I knew she cared, but now I *see* how much."

"You can argue with me all you want, but the way I *see* it . . ."

We instinctively know there's a seeing that goes deeper than informational knowledge, and this seeing transforms vital elements of our personality—our hopes and dreams; our gut feelings; our deeply rooted attitudes, instincts, and motives. Knowing information and responding to it may or may not change our heart. A radically new perspective does.

Embracing a new worldview may be catapulted forward by visual or sensory knowledge, or by seeing in a new way. They say a picture is worth a thousand words—a *million* seems closer to the mark—and is far more memorable too. That's why the Bible is full of stories, parables, and experiences; why God inspired prophets to see visions and illustrate truth in tangible ways; and why he eventually clothed himself in human flesh to live among us. From beginning to end, God gives us images—highly visual and symbolic representations of who he is and what he does. We don't just read his instructions; we see what living out the truth looks like. We don't just read that he is a deliverer; we see numerous examples of dramatic deliverance. He doesn't just tell us he cares for us; he inspires a king to portray him as a shepherd and his Son to dramatize sacrificial, unconditional love in eternally indelible ways. Those pictures and portrayals are life-changing.

If how we live flows out of who we are, being must come before doing. And if *seeing* so profoundly shapes *being*, then having this life-changing vision is vital. It is the key to the transformation we long for—that is, we become what we behold. The Holy Spirit works powerfully on the screens of our minds. We are drawn to whatever we focus on and emulate what we admire. Discipleship that begins with vision flows much more naturally into being and doing. Vision stirs us to be who we're called to be and to live as we're called to live.

The significance of our vision is the premise behind this devotional commentary series. The goal is to embrace a holistic, visual mode of learning. This series assumes that because we, as human beings, live from our identity and follow whatever vision we have, transformation happens by seeing in new ways. Instead of encouraging us simply to *know* and then *do*, the aim of these commentaries is to cast a vision for us to *see*, then *be*, then *live*. Like Jesus, who incorporated visual language into all his teaching, this series aims to refocus our inner eye. If we can see what the biblical writers saw and live according to that vision, we can be transformed.

THE ART OF ENVISIONING

We must train our brains to see and think in new ways. It doesn't just happen. The biblical mandate to renew our minds implies a conscious reorientation of our thought life. Old thought patterns are stubborn; those established neural pathways actively resist new pathways as intruders (which is why New Year's resolutions, exercise and diet plans, and quitting a bad habit can be so difficult). In most areas of life, this neurological dynamic—tapping into our established neural pathways—is helpful; we don't have to relearn everything each day. But when we've been called to reorient the way we think, we have to be relentless about it.

At a practical level, we can greatly amplify this process by (1) recognizing the vision behind biblical texts; (2) immersing ourselves in that vision (declaring the truths of Scripture out loud can help with this, as our brain is very responsive to the sound of our own voice, even if, at first, we don't think we sound convincing); and (3) practicing the art of envisioning.

This latter practice has been somewhat disparaged over the past couple of centuries because we've associated it with "imagination"—as in, "that's *only* your imagination," or "that's just a figment of your imagination," as if our internal vision is no reflection of reality. This would be news to biblical prophets, psalmists, storytellers, and teachers of parables, who all used highly visual language to express truth. Our imagination *can* be used to disengage us from reality—in fact, that's what many people do with it—but it is also our primary means of envisioning truth, which is exactly why God gave us so many stories and images and illustrations. He *wants* us to see his Kingdom—to picture his nature, his purposes, and his work in our lives. It's impossible to read Jesus' parables, study the stories in Acts or in the Old Testament historical books, or read the Psalms and Prophets without developing certain images in our minds. Our lives change when we immerse ourselves in those images.

In envisioning the Kingdom of God and all God's ways, we aren't trying to convince ourselves of something that *isn't* true—simply a figment of our imagination. We're training ourselves in what *is*. Sanctified imagination is not a flight from reality; it's a flight directly into it. We insist that our natural minds, long steeped in limited vision and distorted ways of thinking, must now conform to reality as God defines it.

That's when transformation occurs. When we see God, ourselves, our world, and his Kingdom as he does, we rarely have to discipline ourselves to live differently. We just do it.

IN THIS COMMENTARY

Because this is a *devotional commentary*, you will find material here that fits both descriptors: commentary on the text, and devotional or inspirational thoughts that apply the text to your life, specifically in the ways you see, become transformed, and live out that transformation. In this commentary you will find

- an introduction to the biblical book;
- an introduction for each subsection of the book, explaining its place and purpose in the text, the context or background of that section, and how it fits into the big-picture vision of biblical truth;
- a series of devotionals on the text that
    - further explain context, background, meaning, and purpose,
    - offer suggestions for practical application,
    - inspire and challenge you to *re-envision*—to learn to see in new ways;
- a discussion guide in the back to help you further reflect on the Scripture passages and/or talk about them with others to expand your spiritual vision even more.

As you read, practice the art of envisioning. Pray for Holy Spirit–inspired perspectives. Notice what and how the biblical writers see, and immerse your heart and mind in those visions. Adopt them as your own. More and more, you will enter into the heights and depths of God's Kingdom and live in his ways.

INTRODUCTION TO PHILIPPIANS

Philippi was as Roman as a Macedonian city could get. Ever since 42 BC, when Octavian (the future Caesar Augustus) declared it a colony after a pivotal battle in Rome's civil war, it had been increasingly Romanized. The city was placed under the jurisdiction of Roman law, adopted Latin as its primary language, enjoyed tax-exempt status, and drew numerous Roman soldiers who settled there to live out their retirement. Less diverse than many colonies, Philippi had fewer "easterners" than the more cosmopolitan cities. Jews and Christians were thus small minorities—and were often treated with contempt because of it.

This minority status was apparent when Paul and his ministry companions first visited (Acts 16:11-12). The city had no synagogue, presumably because there were not enough Jewish men to establish one (a quorum of ten was required), so the travelers shared their message with a group of women who had gathered by the river on the Sabbath. But Paul and his companions knew God had led them to this place. Paul had wanted to make further headway in Asia Minor, but God redirected him—first by halting his plans and then by giving him a vision of a Macedonian man calling for help. So the team crossed the upper Aegean Sea and entered this new ministry frontier.

As they ministered throughout the city, they delivered a slave girl from a malicious spirit that was making her a profitable fortune teller, provoking a mob reaction—always dangerous in a Roman colony, risking the city's special privileges. The city magistrates dealt with Paul and Silas harshly, only to find out the next day that they had imprisoned two Roman citizens without a trial—also risky in a Roman colony. At the pleading of the city officials, who recognized their own precarious situation, Paul and his team departed, leaving behind a fledgling congregation in a city very suspicious of its beliefs.

The whole episode highlighted several important aspects of Philippian society—its emphasis on citizenship, its connections with Rome and its military, its disdain for unauthorized or unfamiliar religions, and its pressure on those who didn't fit the culture or who threatened the status quo. Philippian believers had to live against the grain of their culture, as most believers do, and Paul recognized the challenges they were facing.

Years later, most likely when Paul was under house arrest in Rome, he received a gift of financial and moral support from this congregation. And he remembered them fondly. Comments in some of his letters tell us that he had kept in touch with them, and from time to time he had heard from co-workers who had been there. Relative to other young congregations, the church in Philippi was doing well. But it wasn't free of problems. Anytime God begins a new work, there seems to be backlash—opposition from the outside or threats from within. In the case of the Philippian believers, it was some of both.

LIFE AS A PHILIPPIAN CHRISTIAN

Imagine yourself as a believer in Jesus in this first-century church at Philippi. When Paul and his team came through the city, your eyes were opened to the power of God and the message of salvation. Even now, some years later, you still remember the thrill of being part of a new, life-changing movement. But living out an unsanctioned religion in a community that looks down on "eastern" influences—like faith in the Hebrew God and a Jewish Messiah—hasn't been easy. Polytheists and proponents of the imperial cult don't approve of your foreign beliefs, and traveling Jewish teachers—even some who believe in Jesus—don't approve of Gentiles claiming their God without fully embracing his law. In the religious landscape of your city, you're caught between competing forces with high-pressure tactics.

Meanwhile, your small congregation is showing some cracks in its foundation. Some people are in danger of caving to the pressure of the Jewish legalists; two influential women who are at odds with each other are threatening the unity of the fellowship. A visit from your church's founding apostle might help settle things down, but he's under house arrest in Rome, and his fate seems very uncertain.

It would be easy in this kind of situation to get discouraged. From all appearances, the gospel isn't binding people together in close fellowship as it should, and it isn't yet transforming the culture of the city, at least not noticeably. Your fledgling movement still exists under the thumb of imperial authority, Rome's authorized religions, and the eclectic religious culture around you. The universal truth you've believed in appears to be a small light in a vast, dark world.

But that's the problem, isn't it? Things aren't always as they appear. What looks like a position of defeat is really the launching point of a world-transforming faith. What looks like a local dispute will actually become a subject in a letter that profoundly changes people's lives for at least the next two millennia. What seems to be a cacophony of competing beliefs is really the context for sorting out the principles of a faith that will eventually cover the planet and bring glory to God. The Philippians don't yet see the implications of their community of faith. They're stuck in the small picture. They need a bigger, clearer vision.

We all do. How we see God, ourselves, the people around us, and the world itself shapes everything about us. Vision—our microvision of today's responsibilities, our macrovision of our life's purpose, and everything in between—is what drives us. When our hearts are filled with a vision of some possible future, we are inspired to pursue it. But when our eyes are filled only with the problems in front of us, we become easily disheartened—even when those circumstances don't tell the whole story. Everything depends on what we choose to see.

On his first visit to Philippi, as well as on many other occasions, Paul had seen God overrule circumstances and leverage them for powerful purposes. Opposition and "setbacks" catapulted Paul and Silas in their work at Philippi moving forward. Paul was quite familiar with the dynamic of God using a crisis to usher his Kingdom into a situation. The key component in that process was faith—the kind evidenced by Paul and Silas when they worshiped God in prison after being ruthlessly beaten. They were well acquainted with the art of envisioning the truth behind the scenes.

Like all Scripture, Paul's letter to the Philippians reorients our vision. It is clear throughout this letter that he was at peace and that the believers at Philippi weren't. And the difference is perspective. He clearly wanted to change how they viewed their (and his) circumstances. By reframing the picture, he gave them reasons to celebrate, endure, heal their divisions, and move forward in faith. And he gave us a field manual for seeing our lives with new eyes.

PAUL'S POWERFUL RHETORICAL STRATEGY

This letter is a masterpiece in pairing instructions with real-life examples of those instructions. Paul not only teaches the values and attitudes he wants his readers to have; he also demonstrates them. In fact, he explicitly points to himself as a role model in case they happen not to catch the hints, urging them to continue in his instructions (2:12), follow his pattern (3:17), and imitate whatever they saw him doing (4:9).

- Just as Paul had rooted his life in heavenly realities and what ultimately matters (1:21-23; 3:7-14), he encouraged the Philippians to similarly root their lives and focus on their ultimate purpose (1:27; 3:20-21). Both he and the Philippian believers would receive everything they needed not from the resources of the world but from God's riches in glory (4:19).
- Just as Paul consistently and repeatedly chose to rejoice regardless of whatever else was going on (1:3-4, 15-18; 2:17; 4:10), the Philippians were to anchor their lives in joy in every situation (2:18, 29; 3:1; 4:4).
- Just as Paul recognized the big picture and viewed every circumstance, even adversity, positively (1:12-14, 20-26; 3:7-8, 12-14; 4:12-13), he wanted his readers also to focus on the big picture and to see their adversity positively in light of what God was doing in it (1:10, 27-30; 3:15; 4:6-9).
- Like Jesus (2:5-8), Paul had humbled himself in willingness to serve and sacrifice for others (1:1; 2:17; 3:7-8), as had Timothy and Epaphroditus

(2:19-30). Now the Philippians were to follow suit and humble themselves in service and sacrifice for others (2:3-5, 14-15; 4:2), in contrast to certain selfish people Paul mentions (1:17; 2:21; 3:18-19).

- Just as Paul affirmed and honored others, including the Philippians (1:3-8; 2:19-30; 4:1, 14-17), the Philippians were to affirm and honor others (2:3-4, 29).
- Paul had clearly trained his mind not to worry but to think good, hope-filled, joyful thoughts—a pattern he demonstrates in nearly every aspect of the letter but especially in 1:6, 12-26; 3:7-11; and 4:12-13. The Philippians likewise are encouraged to train their minds to think good thoughts and not be anxious (2:2, 14; 4:4-8).
- Just as Paul allowed the affection and compassion of Christ to fill his heart for these believers (1:7-8), they were to feel the affection and compassion of Christ for each other (2:1-4; 4:2-3).

By including both instruction and example, the letter provides words that teach and pictures that demonstrate. Like most of Scripture, Philippians is an exercise in envisioning truth. Paul's goal was that as the Philippians re-envisioned the truth they had first been taught—as they reoriented themselves to the big vision they had embraced as new believers—their lives would be changed.

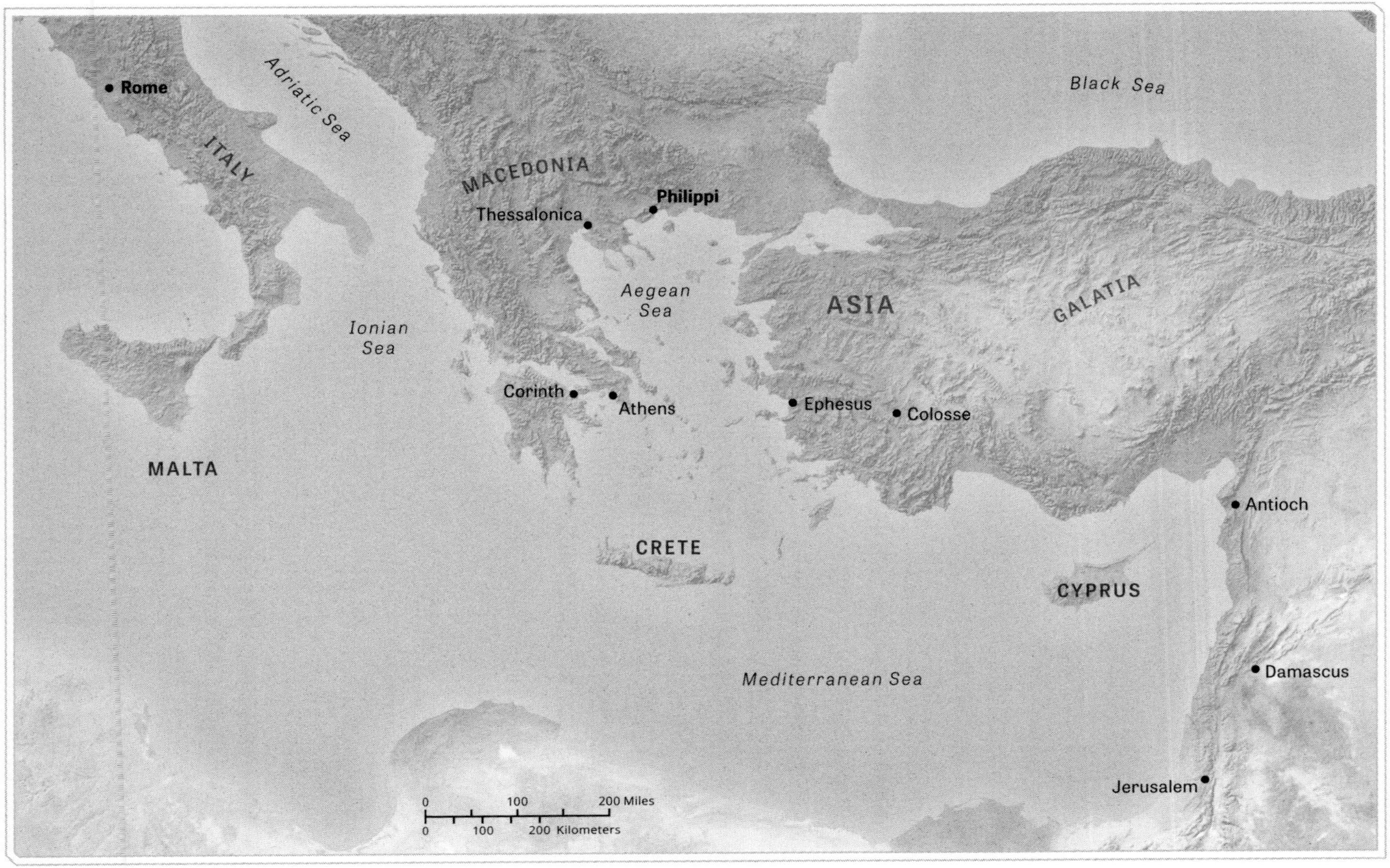
Rome
ITALY
Adriatic Sea
MACEDONIA
Philippi
Thessalonica
Black Sea
Aegean Sea
Ionian Sea
ASIA
GALATIA
Corinth
Athens
Ephesus
Colosse
MALTA
Antioch
CRETE
CYPRUS
Damascus
Mediterranean Sea
Jerusalem
0 100 200 Miles
0 100 200 Kilometers

PHILIPPIANS 1:1-11

RECONNECTIONS

In many respects, the first part of this letter is standard for Paul's letters. Paul identifies himself and Timothy as the authors, greets the Philippians, calls them "God's holy people in Philippi who belong to Christ Jesus," and proceeds to express appreciation for them. While these elements are conventional, they are also filled with unusual warmth. Of all the churches established and overseen by Paul, the Philippian church was relatively problem-free. He seems to have been particularly close to them and remembers them fondly.

BACKGROUND

Under house arrest in Rome, Paul had quite a bit of freedom to receive visitors and correspondence from the outside. The Philippians had sent one of their own, Epaphroditus, to see Paul and deliver a financial gift. One of the reasons

Paul wrote this letter was to acknowledge that gift and show his appreciation for it. He calls them "partners" (1:5), partly because of their history of generosity with him, and partly because he saw them as supportive co-workers who were continuing the mission in Philippi in the years he was away.

But Paul had other reasons for writing too. Epaphroditus had apparently filled him in on some of their troubles—some from outside the fellowship, some from within—and Paul was never short on advice. He understood as well as anyone how to deal with opposition from those outside the community, and he was also well acquainted with friction among those within. The believers needed to know how to navigate such challenges, and he was rather experienced in dealing with them. Chiefly, he wanted them to focus on "what really matters" (1:10). The trivial can easily take center stage, and for some of the Philippians it evidently had.

THE BIG PICTURE

Because love is the foundation of God's Kingdom, relationships are the priority in the Christian life. Paul will address some of the Philippians' relational issues as the letter progresses, but he sets the tone up front by reconnecting with them relationally as their far-away friend who is near in spirit. They had reconnected with him by sending financial support, not as a mere transaction, but as a sign of their affection. In return, he expresses his affection for them.

As Christians, we tend to focus a lot on truth and doctrine, and we can easily push our relational bonds into the background. In this letter, Paul pulls relationship back to the forefront, and he does so in strongly emotional terms. He wants to touch his readers' hearts because that's where love, unity, and ultimate calling are meant to flourish. Regardless of whatever he teaches them and however he corrects them, they need to know that his words are written in the context of a lasting, loving relationship.

A MODEL OF TRUTH

Philippians 1

After a brief salutation and blessing, Paul opens his letter to the Philippians with some affirming words for them and comments about his current situation. On the surface, he seems to be encouraging them in their faith and calming their concerns. But as the letter unfolds, it will become clear that there is much more between the lines here. The apostle who later urges his readers to show their affection for each other, refuse to complain, live as lights in the midst of darkness, rejoice, be anxious for nothing, dwell on what's good and true, and be content in all situations is modeling all these attitudes for them right from the start. He sets himself up as the example of what he will teach them.

At least four issues relayed in this first chapter give Paul an opportunity to be downcast or distraught. He could easily look at the division in the Philippian church, his own confinement, rival preachers who are jockeying for spiritual status, and the possibility of his execution as the basis for a negative outlook. He could be angry about the factions that seem to be developing, be outraged over the injustice of his situation, criticize the self-promoting teachers, and fear for his own life.

Instead, he emphasizes the positive in each of these circumstances: Yes, the Philippians are in a growth process, but God will certainly bring them to maturity. Sure, his imprisonment is unfair, but God is reaching people who otherwise would not be reached. True, the rivalrous preachers have impure motives, but they are still getting the name of Jesus out there. And yes, Paul might die, but it's still a win-win situation—he will either be with Christ or bear more fruit. In spite of all the apparent crises, Paul is relentlessly hopeful.

Why? Because he sees who God is. He has a clear vision of God's nature and character, and he interprets everything in light of that vision. Because he knows who he is in Christ and how faithful God is to his promises, Paul can simply rejoice and trust that God is powerfully at work in everything—even when other observers see nothing but trouble.

When we have a skewed vision of God, we see our captivities, adversaries, and setbacks as referendums on whether we are in good standing with him. *Did I step out of his will? Am I being disciplined? Are my prayers falling on deaf ears? Where is the promise of divine favor?* Our experiences become the criteria by which we interpret God. Or to put it another way, we see God through the lens of our circumstances.

We see none of this with Paul. He was well trained in the art of seeing circumstances through the lens of God. Lest we think he had some sort of advantage as a superapostle, we need only to look back at his original experience in Philippi—the confusing journey to this new frontier, the unexpected absence of a synagogue, the riot that led to his beating and imprisonment, and the legal dispute with city magistrates. In all these potentially disorienting experiences, in spite of the tyranny of circumstances, Paul had seen God come through again and again. He had learned to read between the lines of his surroundings and envision the bigger picture.

That's our calling, too, and Paul models it for us just as clearly as he did for the Philippian believers. We can stop second-guessing our situations and trust that God is working in them. He is unequivocally faithful to his people. When we see that, we, too, become rejoicing, grateful observers of his unfolding purposes in our lives.

RE-ENVISION GOD

If you aren't certain of God's kindness and faithfulness to you, much of what happens in your life will cause fear and anxiety. Insecurity about your life reflects insecurity with him. But he has already declared you to be secure in him. He is *for* you (Romans 8:31). If he has promised to work all things for the good of his people, then all things are redeemable. Learn to see him at work in every situation to fulfill this promise. Notice the good he is accomplishing and trust him to complete it. You will face adversity, setbacks, and losses in life, but even the worst are lined with strong elements of hope. Like Paul, learn to worship in the darkest places, and the light will become clear in the midst of them.

A HOLY IDENTITY

I am writing to all of God's holy people in Philippi who belong to Christ Jesus.

1:1

As ancient letters go, the opening to Philippians is pretty conventional. Paul (with Timothy) greets the people he is writing to and offers a blessing of grace and peace. But the way he addresses his recipients is anything but conventional. He doesn't just address the Philippians as believers or members of a congregation. He addresses them as holy. Saints. Those who belong to Jesus.

This address is a huge statement of identity, and Paul uses it often with the recipients of his letters, even in contexts where those recipients aren't acting particularly holy. Rather than urging his readers to become holy, to live as those who belong to Jesus—in other words, to strive toward that identity—he insists that it's already true. The old nature is no longer their true self. He never encourages his readers to become something they are not; he wants them to grow into the new nature they have been given and live according to who they already are.

Many believers reverse the order. We receive our salvation through faith in Christ and then try to prove to ourselves that we're saved. We aim to establish ourselves as sons or daughters of God rather than realizing that we are already sons and daughters who can live from that assurance. We're trying to become "somebody" in the Kingdom because we don't recognize that we're somebody from the start—we are the objects of God's infinite, extravagant love. You can't get any higher than that. Yet most of us keep trying to reach higher.

This never works. People who try to become holy, assuming they aren't already, are always working at it, feeling as if they are constantly falling short, and burning out. People who know they are already holy—not perfect or sinless, but cleansed by Jesus' blood, empowered by his Spirit, and set apart for God's purposes—live from a place of rest and experience greater change.

Understanding our identity is vital. We have to know who we are before we try to figure out what to do. Our thoughts, words, and actions flow from our sense of identity; we always live out the vision we have of ourselves. If, for example, we see ourselves merely as struggling sinners—the emphasis of much teaching throughout church history that acknowledges salvation by grace but stresses our sinfulness—we will inevitably live out that vision and continue to struggle with sin. It's important to know what we were saved *from* and be thankful for it, but we will remain there if we don't also have a vision of what we were saved *for*. Throughout Scripture, before we are told what to do, we are told who we are: holy and beloved, adopted sons and daughters of God, citizens of a heavenly realm.

RE-ENVISION YOURSELF

If you don't view yourself as holy, as a saint who irrevocably belongs to Jesus, you'll find it impossible to live out that identity. You have to see who you are in order to experience that reality. There's no need to strive for that identity; it was already settled at the Cross. Your identity is not defined by your decisions, habits, character flaws, track record, or any other experience. It's defined by God. Embrace it in confidence. See yourself as holy and pure, set apart for his special purposes, and begin walking in that truth.

THE ATTITUDE OF PRAYER

Every time I think of you, I give thanks to my God. . . . I make my requests for all of you with joy.

1:3-4

Near the end of this letter, Paul will cast a vision for a life at peace. He will emphasize changed attitudes, mental habits, and ways of approaching prayer. But he knows these believers need to see what anxiety-free, grateful prayers look like in situations like theirs. Instructions without examples aren't always helpful, so he gives them a demonstration up front.

In fact, the whole first chapter of the letter demonstrates the instructions given in the fourth chapter. Paul is presenting a vision of how to see and think differently—not as the world thinks, critically and pessimistically or in fear or dread, but filled with hope in light of what God is doing to fulfill his promises of abundant life and advance his Kingdom on earth. When we see from a Kingdom perspective, we have a lot to celebrate.

Paul's gratitude and joy tell us quite a bit about how he viewed prayer. Requests, by nature, imply that something is lacking or some change is needed. Joy and gratitude demonstrate that the lack or need, even when very real, is not a cause for discouragement. Paul is not offering desperate prayers here, with a slim hope that God might respond. His attitude reflects full confidence that his requests are going to be answered. Faith always assumes God's goodness.

Don't miss the importance of this. Paul attaches joy to his prayers *not* because he sees things turning in the right direction. They aren't—yet. He has heard of division within the church and opposition from the outside. These are significant contradictions to what he is praying. It would be easy to wonder why God isn't responding, but Paul doesn't let his mind go where ours often does. God *is* answering his prayers, regardless of the contradictions he sees, and Paul has to make a choice: accept what his natural eyes see or trust that God is working out his purposes, not just vaguely or theoretically, but specifically. The Philippians are growing in maturity. God will make sure of that, even if some people in the congregation are behaving immaturely or entertaining false teachings.

Every prayer is a cause for joy because it invites God into our circumstances. Whether God answers exactly as we expect isn't the issue; his presence in any situation brings solutions and peace for those who believe. Prayer gives us access to the always-available, life-transforming gifts of supernatural wisdom, power, and love.

RE-ENVISION PRAYER

Do you see prayer as a requisition for an all-or-nothing answer or as an invitation for God to show up? The first approach stakes everything on a specific outcome and may set you up for disappointment. The second expects God to invade the situation to accomplish something good, which he certainly will, and prompts a celebration in advance.

Notice the energy behind your prayers—whether it's joy or anxiety. In every prayer, you are filling your vision either with God's promises and faithfulness or with the contradictions your natural eyes see. Which is more reliable? In your moments of asking, your joy will tell you a lot about what you actually believe.

PARTICIPANTS IN THE KINGDOM

You have been my partners in spreading the Good News about Christ from the time you first heard it until now.

1:5

Paul had various partners throughout his missionary journeys. Acts mentions Barnabas and John Mark, then Silas and Timothy. Luke accompanied him on portions of his travels. Paul wrote of Aquila, Priscilla, and Titus as fellow workers, and according to references and greetings in his letters, his ministry intersected with numerous other helpers and collaborators along the way. He may have been a strong leader, but he never saw himself as independent. He relied on many partners.

Here he includes the Philippians among them. Paul had visited Philippi at least twice (Acts 16:11-40; 20:1-6) and had received gifts and correspondence from them on several occasions (Philippians 4:16). But they were a community of new believers anchored in their own city, a Roman colony attached to its Roman ways. They were lights shining in a dark world (2:15), facing opposition from the outside (1:28; 3:2), and dealing with some degree of internal conflict (2:1-4; 4:2-4). They were certainly a work in progress, yet it was not an iffy progress. Paul was certain of what God was accomplishing in them (1:6). Despite distance from him and their level of spiritual maturity—greater than most of his churches but still somewhat young in the faith—he considered them partners in his work. From the start, they were participants in advancing the Kingdom.

Everything Paul and the Philippian believers were going through fit into this vision. He did not see any adversity or opposition as too big for them or their mission. He will describe much of that adversity in the verses and chapters ahead, but none of it is ultimately threatening. God's people were growing, the Good News was spreading, and the Kingdom was advancing. Nothing could quench the fruit of the gospel.

RE-ENVISION PROGRESS

When your life is consumed with one goal, you interpret everything in light of that goal. Paul saw everything in light of the progress of the Kingdom in the lives of God's people and the communities they lived in, and he will spend much of this letter imparting that vision to his readers. If your one goal is to have a nice life, the kinds of situations that come up in this letter will feel threatening. If your one goal is to love and pursue the Lord with all your heart, they won't be. Adverse circumstances become just a means to an end.

We can be absorbed with the situations right in front of us, as is our tendency. Or, like Paul, we can adjust the focus until the details of those situations are blurred and the lives of God's people and his mission in this world are sharp and clear. That's a vision that redefines progress and reveals other believers for who they are: participants in the Kingdom, partners in the mission, companions in an everlasting fellowship. That gives meaning to every relationship and adds depth to everything we do.

A VIEW FROM THE END

I am certain that God, who began the good work within you, will continue his work until it is finally finished on the day when Christ Jesus returns.

1:6

It's only natural to base our opinions of people on our experiences. Our relationships have a history—we see character and personality in people's interactions with us and others. We recognize the tone of their words, see the expressions on their faces, and experience the consequences of their decisions. We enjoy being around them (or not) because of the way they treat us. We base our opinions of them almost entirely on the past.

This is what Paul called "evaluating others from a human point of view" in another letter, where he urged a different approach (2 Corinthians 5:16). It isn't that our observations aren't true; our perceptions are often right on target. But they don't define who a person is. If every believer in Christ is a new creation, an entirely new person for whom old things have passed away and "a new life has begun" (2 Corinthians 5:17), then the truth about them is not who they have been but who they are becoming. We have to learn to see people according to their destiny and calling.

That's essentially Paul's view of the Philippian believers. He loves them and appreciates his experiences with them, but he knows they aren't perfect. In fact, some of them, as we will see, have become a little self-focused and contentious. If these characteristics defined them, he would be less thankful and joyful. Instead, he has learned to see people as being in the midst of transformation, knowing they are different from who they used to be but not yet fully formed into who they are going to be. He refuses to focus on their shortcomings because he knows the Spirit is at work in them. God will finish what he started.

We have to learn to see people that way too—to envision their future as fully transformed people in Christ. What we see now is part of the process, not the end result. Amazing things happen when we start treating people according to their future; they often begin to grow into it.

RE-ENVISION OTHERS

God does not see you according to your past but according to your future. He looks at you through the lens of Christ. You have found your identity in him by faith and are therefore a new creation. He already sees the fullness of your maturity and future glory.

If this is God's perspective of you, it's also his perspective of other believers. You can align your vision with his by choosing to see people as fully mature and transformed. No matter that they haven't gotten there on the timeline yet; God finishes what he starts, so they will.

Try an experiment in one of your more difficult relationships. Picture the person as fully mature in Christ, fulfilling their calling and exercising their gifts you see in them. Hold that vision in your mind as you speak to them and let it shape your attitude toward them. You may find that this person begins to step into the picture you've envisioned. Treating people according to who they are becoming rather than who they have been transforms relationships and gives them the grace and space to grow.

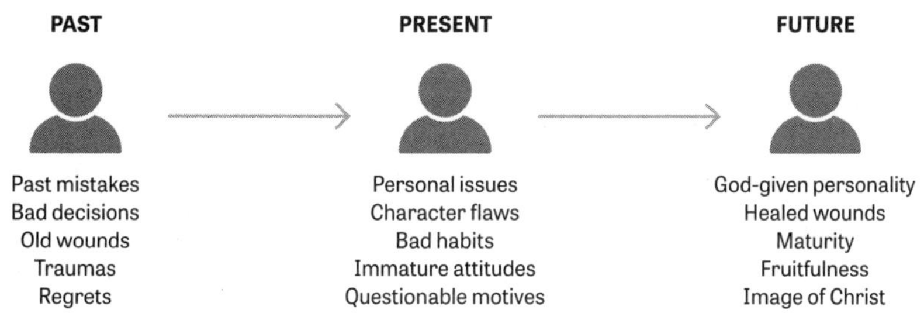

A choice of focus: Most people see others (and themselves) according to past and present personas and respond critically, based on shortcomings and flaws. God does address human sin and imperfection, and we can too, but he views people (including us) according to our future, values us for who we are becoming, responds affirmingly, and calls us to do the same.

You have a special place in my heart. . . . God knows how much I love you and long for you with the tender compassion of Christ Jesus.

1:7-8

Counselors have long been aware of an interesting yet disturbing phenomenon: People who grow up with emotionally distant fathers tend to see God as distant. Those raised by unreliable fathers tend to struggle with faith. Those whose fathers exerted strong, authoritarian discipline tend to see God as ready to punish whoever steps out of line. The images we receive from our parents or authority figures shape our perception of God's nature, for better or worse.

That is one reason so many people embrace the theological truth of God's love without sensing it or experiencing it deep in their hearts. To hearts and minds that long ago insulated themselves from tender affection, his love is just a principle or doctrine. A surprising number of Christians find it easy to tell others that God loves them while never fully basking in God's love for themselves. Many of us end up with a perception that God loves us because it's his nature, or his divine job description, not because he actually wants to. The ability to think *God delights in me! He not only loves me; he likes me!* is rarer than our theology says it should be.

Paul makes it clear to the Philippians that his love for them is not obligatory. He longs for them with tender affection. He has deep compassion for them. They have moved his heart to overflow with gratitude and joy. And to show that this is not just one man's feelings, he attributes his affection and compassion to the Spirit of Jesus within him. Paul delights in these friends because God himself delights in them.

In another letter, Paul profoundly describes love in words that still resonate in many people's hearts (1 Corinthians 13). John would later write that God *is* love (1 John 4:8, 16). We're told that God sent his Son because he loved the world (John 3:16), that love is the centerpiece of the greatest commandments (Matthew 22:34-40), and that Jesus' love for his followers is the basis of their love for each other (John 13:34). In other words, divine love is the foundation of our entire salvation and fullness of life. We can't experience genuine fulfillment, growth, or fruitfulness unless we immerse ourselves in it.

Until we do, we will interpret correction (as Paul is about to give to the Philippians) as condemnation. We will misjudge the Father's heart toward us and question whether his will for us and his answers to our prayers (like those Paul has just prayed) are really in our best interests. We'll see circumstances (as Paul is about to spell out) as threats to our well-being rather than catalysts for it. Without the backdrop of absolute assurance of divine love, many of the circumstances of our lives look worrisome.

RE-ENVISION GOD'S LOVE

Like Paul, learn to see yourself as both a receiver and carrier of God's love. Open your spirit to the affection of Christ and let him stir in you affection for those around you. This is the heart of discipleship, of relationships, and of life itself.

When you imagine God gazing at you, can you see him smile? Is there delight in his eyes? If not, this needs to become the focus of your relationship with him. Pray for a revelation of his overwhelming love. You cannot give what you have not received for yourself. Receiving his affection—directly and through other believers—reorients your entire vision. Let it fill you up and overflow into the lives of those around you.

SENSING GOD'S HEART

I pray that your love will overflow more and more, and that you will keep on growing in knowledge and understanding.

1:9

Paul boldly claimed in the previous verse that his feelings for the Philippians came from Jesus, or at least reflected Jesus' affection for them. His heart and the Lord's were in sync. That notion challenges the thinking of many modern Christians. We have no objection to aligning our minds with God's Word, but our emotions? Feelings are so unreliable, aren't they? Yet Scripture testifies throughout to God's emotions, and the prophets, Jesus, and Paul all demonstrate that we can share those emotions with him. Not only can we have the mind of Christ (1 Corinthians 2:16); we can also have his heart.

Synchronizing with God's heart is a substantial part of our discipleship. Relationships generally don't grow deeper through shared knowledge, but they do grow deeper through shared emotional responses. God calls us to love what he loves, hate what he hates, rejoice when he rejoices, have compassion where he has compassion, grieve where he grieves, and more. We cannot grow to be like Jesus unless our hearts align with his.

So Paul urged the Philippians to let their love—Jesus' love—overflow, just as it overflowed from Paul's heart toward these believers. In fact, in a reversal from what we might expect, the flow of love would serve to increase their knowledge and understanding. Their hearts were the priority; their minds would follow.

RE-ENVISION HUMAN LOVE

When we learn what's possible in Scripture—here, to have the heart of Jesus just as we have his mind—we have a choice. We can view that possibility as an invitation, or we can view it as an exception that might not apply to us. God honors those who go for it. Those who seek to align their hearts with God's, sensing his emotions, attitudes, sentiments, and perspectives, will find themselves growing into his likeness in surprisingly new ways. What was once a matter of knowing his Word and doing it turns into a shared experience of loving, rejoicing, having compassion, grieving, delighting, and celebrating. The disciplines of the Spirit become much easier when we share his heart.

The more we experience God's love, the better we can give it. Those who see that they are deeply, irrevocably, passionately, eternally loved begin to overflow with the same love. They stop trying to earn it, achieve it, fabricate it, or substitute it with counterfeits. Their search for full acceptance ends, and they are free to pour it out. They catch a vision of the Father's heart and want everyone to experience it.

Prioritize receiving the Father's love in ever-increasing measure. Immerse yourself in it, bask in it, and let it saturate your heart. As you do, your heart will align with his, and love will flow. You will begin to see people as God sees them, and your heart will beat with his.

LIVING IN THE BIG PICTURE

I want you to understand what really matters, so that you may live pure and blameless lives until the day of Christ's return.

1:10

Paul and Silas had been beaten with bone-bruising rods, chained in shackles that were designed both to secure captives and intensify their pain, and left in prison in the dark of night (Acts 16). Yet they worshiped loudly enough for other prisoners to hear and stuck around even after God had provided a miraculous deliverance. They did not resist arrest, threaten the officials with retaliation, or, as far as we know, complain about their predicament. Clearly they were focused on something other than their own unjust treatment.

Most of us live life somewhere within the frame of a small picture. We focus on what matters to us, how the details of our lives are working out, and what we can do to improve our situation. We may even do so with the intent of bearing fruit for God's Kingdom—but perhaps not always with an awareness of how we fit into the grand scheme of things.

Meanwhile, that grand scheme unfolding on all around us. We live in a much bigger picture. Paul and Silas were able to worship and linger because they had a larger vision: what God was doing to advance their mission, how the beating and imprisonment might have created a platform for something greater, how God had his heart set on a jailer's salvation, and more. They knew better than to see their situation as a setback.

Paul's comment in 1:10 reflects the same big-picture awareness. He wants the Philippians to "understand what really matters"—in this case, the love that undergirds the Philippians' faith and all their relationships. To the extent they are bickering with each other or promoting themselves, they are living in the small picture. Submitting all personal agendas to the grand vista of divine love restores the right perspective—a case he will soon make in the following chapter. God is always up to something greater than our immediate circumstances seem to suggest.

RE-ENVISION WHAT MATTERS

If the story of God's Kingdom were a play, where would you fit on the stage? You might initially minimize your role—after all, it's an epic, history-shaping play—but avoid that temptation. Your role is vital. But it's still one of many. The playwright is crafting a narrative that foregrounds his glory and redemptive plan, and the part you play can only be interpreted in light of the whole.

It's easy in the day-to-day grind to lose sight of the whole, but it's there. One day when you look back over your years, you won't remember everything on your to-do list or even all your accomplishments. You will, however, remember your relationships and the love that went into them. So major on what really matters. Beyond your immediate circumstances, see the Author at work. Live with the understanding—and expectation—that he is doing great things for you, in you, and through you every day.

May you always be filled with the fruit of your salvation—the righteous character produced in your life by Jesus Christ—for this will bring much glory and praise to God.

1:11

Centuries of Christian preaching have largely defined the concept of righteousness by what it isn't. It isn't impurity, greed, lust, selfishness, anger, injustice, dishonesty, violence, immorality, or sin of any kind. We assume that if all those sins are absent, righteousness remains. All we have to do is avoid them to live righteously.

But Paul has already pointed to the fruit of salvation without even mentioning sin. He has identified truth, compassion, joy, and love as characteristics of Kingdom life. Righteousness does involve freedom from sin—Paul urged these believers to be pure and blameless in the previous verse—but it's so much more than that. It isn't just the absence of evil; it's the presence of God's character and nature within us.

We can't be righteous unless we actually have God's presence within us. We can act righteously for a time, but we can't be transformed into his image. No amount of discipline or knowledge will accomplish that. We need him to change us.

The good news is that Christ and his righteousness are already there, gifts we've already received. God declares us righteous when we believe Jesus and accept his sacrifice and his righteousness on our behalf. But in practice, growing into that righteousness is a process, a matter of recognizing Jesus within us and relying on him. The Philippians were in the midst of that process. Paul was confident that God would continue working in them until Jesus' return (1:6), but they needed some encouragement. Paul gave plenty of it, and hardly any was about getting rid of sin. His letter was filled with descriptions of the character of Jesus and of his Kingdom. The Philippians' righteousness would be defined not by the absence of sin but by who they were becoming. They were being transformed into the image of Christ.

RE-ENVISION RIGHTEOUSNESS

If you're looking for righteousness simply by avoiding sin, expand your vision. Fill your life with Jesus—his love, compassion, kindness, truth, justice, joy, humility, servant-heartedness, boldness, purity, and peace—and choose not to honor sin by focusing on it. God has not called us to a sin-focused life. He has, however, called us to be filled with his Spirit. Fellowship with him in the depths of our being marginalizes anything that doesn't fit. Or, as Paul put it in another letter, "Walk by the Spirit, and you will not gratify the desires of the flesh" (Galatians 5:16, NIV). When we saturate ourselves in the Righteous One, unrighteousness fades away.

When we fix our gaze on our sin, even in an effort to get rid of it, its hold on us grows stronger. But when we fix our gaze on Jesus, sin begins to lose its grip. Growing in the fruit of our salvation still takes time, but it's driven by the image of the Righteous One within us. Beholding him transforms us, bringing glory and praise to God.

PHILIPPIANS 1:12-18

WHEN IN ROME

After the salutation and words of gratitude, prayer, and appreciation, Paul writes of his own experiences in Rome, perhaps to relieve any concerns the Philippians may have had about him, but perhaps also to demonstrate the power of a true perspective. He is "in chains" for Jesus, he tells them (1:13)—probably a figure of speech, as being under house arrest would usually not involve chains, though he surely felt very restricted. But even from that position, he remains quite active in ministry. He tells them about his ministry, as good friends share news about themselves, but he is also doing something more. The Philippians need to see what it's like for someone to be in a difficult situation without questioning one's calling, growing depressed about one's problems, or becoming critical of one's adversaries. Paul displays that he has none of those attitudes—very purposefully—before addressing some of the challenges the Philippians were facing.

BACKGROUND

Paul was in Rome because he had been at the center of a firestorm in Jerusalem about three years earlier and had been awaiting trial ever since. After watching one procurator leave and another come, without resolution to his case, he appealed to Caesar—a right of citizens, though with huge implications, including a lengthy, cumbersome, expensive process. Yet this appeal got him to Rome, the power center of the empire, where Paul had long felt called to visit (Romans 1:13-15). Though marginalized as a prisoner, he was nevertheless at the epicenter of the Mediterranean world.

Paul's imprisonment could have been an enormous setback to the advance of the gospel, and many observers probably thought it was. Some may have even celebrated the fact. But it wasn't quite fact. Paul was still sharing his faith, and in some highly influential places. And others were preaching the gospel, perhaps even more motivated by Paul's captivity (albeit with some selfish agendas mixed in). Paul's words about the palace guard (Philippians 1:13) might have been particularly comforting to many Philippians, as former guardsmen often retired to places like Philippi and some believers might have had sons, brothers, or nephews serving in Rome. These connections made Paul's interest in sharing his experiences with them all the more encouraging.

THE BIG PICTURE

Some of the Philippians seem to have been living with a small vision, and it conflicted with their big vision. Perhaps they were focused on immediate issues—doing instead of being, proving their point rather than loving God and each other, not recognizing just how vital joy was for their lives, fellowship, and witness. Joy is vastly more important than getting our way or being right, far more important than most people think, and is the strongest antidote to the anxiety and conflict we experience. Most of all, it is a defining characteristic of the environment of heaven. Paul effusively demonstrates it here and throughout this letter.

Unless we see things correctly and line up our immediate vision with our ultimate vision, things won't click. We won't be content (much less joyful), we'll get tossed around and anxious in the storms that come our way, we'll be more prone to conflict, and we'll be unsettled when things don't appear to be going right. Paul repeatedly presents and demonstrates the right vision in this letter. The big picture should always incorporate the small picture, never the other way around.

SEEING THROUGH THE RIGHT LENS

Everything that has happened to me here has helped to spread the Good News.

1:12

On the surface, "everything that has happened" to Paul in his captivity paints a depressing picture. He can't travel where he wants to go, visit churches he wants to visit, preach in synagogues or open forums, or even defend himself unless the opportunity is granted to him. His rivals might be rejoicing that he has been sidelined (see 1:17), and his allies could easily become disheartened. He is dependent on other people for support and communication. Things don't look good for him.

Beneath the surface, however, Paul sees a different picture. God is using Paul and his circumstances to advance the gospel. Paul is writing letters that will inspire many people—he has no idea how many and for how long—with eternal truth. He understands that his captivity is putting him in position to influence key figures in Roman government and society. As far as Paul is concerned, things are looking pretty good.

This contrast in perspectives is a prime example of seeing circumstances through the lens of God rather than seeing God through the lens of circumstances. When we let our immediate situation dictate our experience of God, our vision becomes skewed. We begin to question his heart toward us, his will for our lives, and our own standing with him. Over time, circumstances begin to define our theology—or, more pointedly, our God—and it's always a distorted picture. But when we look at our circumstances in light of God—his presence, power, and purposes—we know they don't tell the whole story. We can envision God working through them or in spite of them. The first perspective undermines our faith every step of the way. The second builds it up.

It's worth noting that Paul has chosen here to focus on how the Kingdom of God is advancing rather than on how the Kingdom is *not* advancing. He is not at all interested in a negative spin. We can be fairly certain that if he were around today, he would not be glued to the steady stream of disturbing or controversial news from our media, with its ratings dependent on crises, outrage, and fear. He would be focused instead on what God is doing, on how the percentage of the world's people who claim the name of Christ is higher now than at any point in history, on how vibrant, Spirit-led movements are proclaiming Jesus and the gospel of grace (regardless of differing theological nuances), and on how the gospel is reaching even impossible-to-reach people in "closed" countries.

In the eyes of many, the world is getting worse and worse. In the eyes of others, the Kingdom is growing more and more. The letter to the Philippians is very clear on which emphasis is appropriate for a citizen of heaven. For those who will soon be instructed to fix their thoughts on what is true and lovely and admirable (4:8), this is a great place to start.

RE-ENVISION CIRCUMSTANCES

Your perspective is a choice. You can fill your heart and mind with what should or should not be happening and wring your hands over the way the world, your life, or anything else happens to be going. Or you can fill your heart and mind with the God who has promised that the increase of his Kingdom will never end, that he will work all things together for your good, and that every situation is filled with redemptive possibilities. You'll find that one perspective inevitably leads to anxiety, fear, outrage, despair, and/or depression. The other leads to gratitude and joy—the overarching themes of this letter. Shifting your thoughts from the old view to the new may take practice and persistence. But it will certainly fill you with hope.

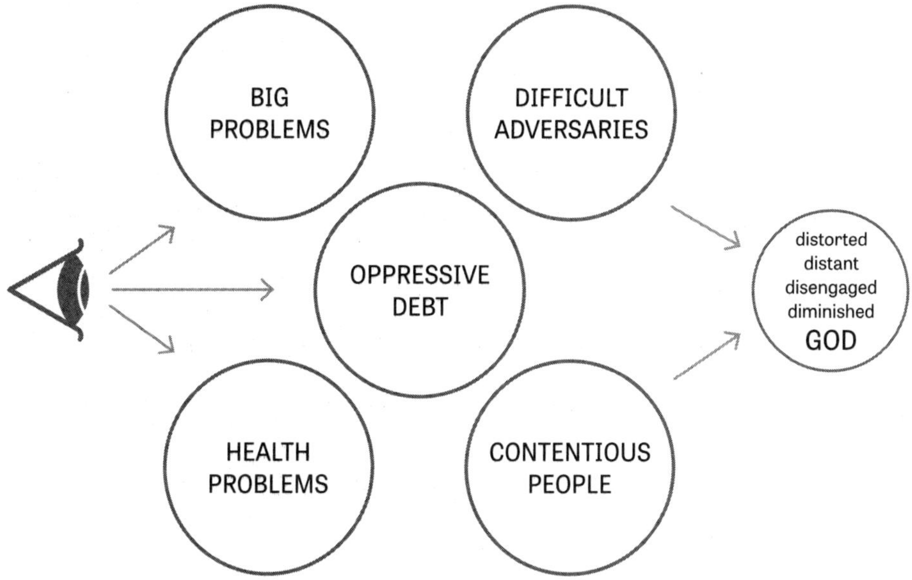

Looking through the right lens: When we see God through the lenses of our circumstances, he appears distant and detached, and our circumstances appear huge. When we see our circumstances through the lens of God, he is magnified in our hearts and minds, and our circumstances resume their true appearance. Our faith weakens or strengthens according to the lenses we look through.

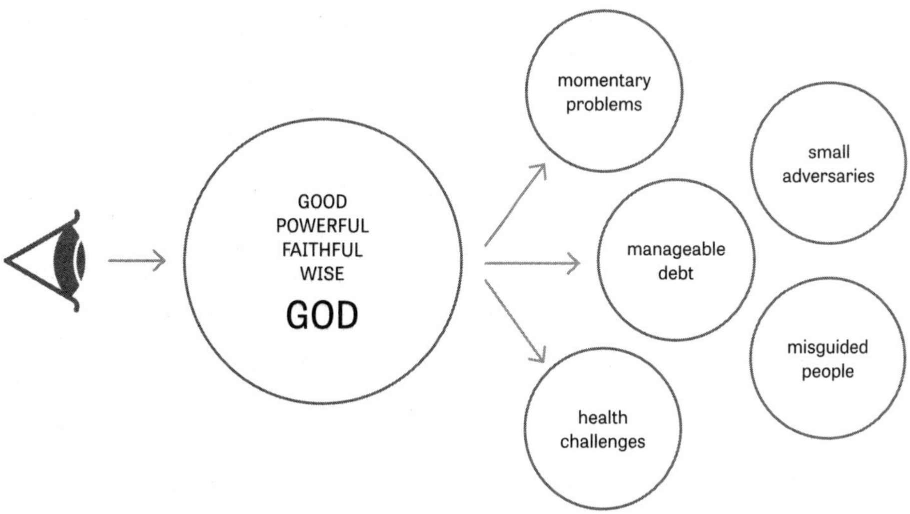

Everyone here, including the whole palace guard, knows that I am in chains because of Christ. And because of my imprisonment, most of the believers here have gained confidence and boldly speak God's message without fear.

1:13-14

The apostle to the Gentile world had been rendered immobile, but that didn't stop him from preaching. His testimony comes up repeatedly in Acts because he was never hesitant to tell it, especially to rulers, administrators, and guards—the same company he was now keeping in his confinement. His wretched circumstances had become a platform for reaching people who were otherwise isolated from the gospel. Paul flipped the script on the concept of a captive audience; the captors became the audience for a man on a mission.

As previously mentioned, these captors in Rome may have been of particular interest to the Philippian believers, as Philippi was a community where many soldiers who had once served in the Praetorian Guard had retired. Anyone in the Philippian church who was a mother, father, aunt, or uncle of a current guard would have wanted to know that the gospel was reaching their ranks. And by Paul's own account, it was. The testimony created by the apostle's suffering was spreading. It served as a demonstration of the bigger picture, an example of someone so rooted in the eternal realm that temporary captivity becomes yet another stage for the divine drama. *If this guy is so unrattled by his situation*, guards and officials must have thought, *if he's so convinced of this Savior he keeps talking about, maybe, just maybe, it's true.* His adversity had become an opportunity.

We need to capture Paul's persistence and his perspective. He lived in a world in which believers in Jesus were a marginalized and minuscule percentage of the empire's (and Philippi's) population, yet he was encouraged by the advance of the Kingdom. We now live in a world in which more than two billion people claim the name of Christ, yet many believers grow more discouraged and defeated by the day. Paul envisioned a Kingdom steadily growing toward ultimate victory. Somehow we've gotten the impression that we're losing the battle and headed toward some domination of godlessness. The difference in visions is stark. Paul would not be looking at today's world the way we do.

Adversity becomes opportunity and perspectives brighten when we (1) see how God is working in the situation (or simply trust that he is) and (2) understand the value of sacrifice. Scripture presents a consistent picture of heaven's fire falling on a worthy sacrifice—at least figuratively, and sometimes literally (for example, Leviticus 9:24; 1 Kings 18:38; 2 Chronicles 7:1)—which means our offerings of suffering or even of inconvenience carry profound spiritual power. God does not waste our trials, especially those willingly endured for the sake of his Kingdom. When we believe he honors our sacrifices, we endure all the more willingly—and live in victory even when the world calls us captives.

RE-ENVISION ADVERSITY

Take your cues from Paul. If his priority had been himself—self-preservation or a personal agenda—he would have already lost. His situation would have rendered the verdict. But with Christ as his priority, he couldn't lose. His vision thrived because Jesus was still alive and active in furthering his Kingdom.

Nothing has changed. Jesus always has been and always will be alive and active in furthering his Kingdom. If you've staked your grand vision for life on that truth, your vision is invincible. You cannot lose. God makes every pain and sacrifice fruitful in the place you offer it.

Some are preaching out of jealousy and rivalry. But others preach about Christ with pure motives.

1:15

Some advocates for the Christian faith were stepping up their efforts in light of Paul's imprisonment. He was never the only person advancing the gospel among Gentiles, and these others knew they were needed now more than ever. Some were capitalizing on his imprisonment to assert their own agendas and build their own reputations. Perhaps they wanted to be seen as leaders of the church or to make a name for themselves with innovative methods that weren't particularly effective. Regardless, Paul was able to find something to celebrate (see 1:18).

If we constantly measure others by the perfection of God, they will always fall short. We will always notice their imperfections, impurities, and incompleteness. Even if they preach and teach effectively, serve others well, work hard, have sincere hearts, and try to build solid relationships, there will always be something more they could have done, or some better outcome they could have achieved. They're human beings in process, after all, and they aren't yet fully mature and complete. Next to God's perfection, they never measure up.

But if we focus instead on what God is doing in their lives—how he is maturing them, bearing fruit through them, encouraging them, demonstrating his patience and perseverance in them, and anything else he might be accomplishing—we can affirm and commend his work in and through them. God's highest and best standard for us—being fully conformed to the image of Christ—is theologically true, but it isn't our whole story. The journey to get there matters. Life isn't a matter of "perfection or bust." If people are heading in the right direction on that journey—if any progress has been made, no matter how small—we can celebrate.

RE-ENVISION GOD'S WORK

In many respects, this choice of perspective is like looking at a glass as half-empty or half-full. And it applies to how we view ourselves as well as others. If we focus primarily on the ways we've fallen short, we'll end up frustrated, burned out, and with horrible self-esteem. If we celebrate even the small things God is doing in us, we can be encouraged and at peace. Whatever we focus on grows larger—in this case, not only in our perceptions but also in our experiences. When we choose to see God at work, his work takes root in us and becomes fruitful.

Recasting our vision to what God has done, is doing, and will continue to do is profoundly encouraging and uplifting. It allows us to see anyone, even ourselves, as pilgrims progressing, just as Paul affirms with the Philippians (1:6). Paul knows God will continue his work in them, and he can trust that God will work even through those teachers preaching with impure motives. He can celebrate any evidence of the gospel advancing, no matter how inconsistently, because he knows God will accomplish his purposes on earth—even through imperfect people.

BEYOND PETTINESS

Whether their motives are false or genuine, the message about Christ is being preached either way, so I rejoice.

1:18

Believers in Rome were being vocal about the gospel, some of them for all the right reasons. Paul's resolve in the face of adversity has actually boosted their confidence (1:14), and they have fearlessly taken up the message because they love him (1:16). Others, however, have seen his confinement as an opportunity to assert themselves. They apparently want Paul's reputation without also having his commission.

Those preaching out of jealousy and rivalry are prime examples of people who have received Christ but are still trying to be "somebody" in the Kingdom of God. Perhaps they don't know their identity as beloved children of God and are striving to prove their worth—as if their ministry exploits will prove to people that Paul isn't the only great leader. *We can be great leaders too!* they seem to say as they take the stage. Their message isn't necessarily wrong; it's just driven by the wrong motives. They are still seeking status in the Kingdom that has already conferred the highest status on all its citizens from day one.

Paul acknowledges the flawed motivations of these look-at-me preachers, but he doesn't condemn them. He understands—from his own experience—that God works through deeply flawed people. As we've seen, he envisions a world in which the Kingdom is advancing and sees a church that is growing toward complete maturity—even though, on both counts, he is confronted with plenty of contrary evidence. Part of that advance is the preaching of people Paul doesn't necessarily like or agree with. There are times in other letters when he emphasizes the importance of a leader's character; but here, instead of seeing his rivals and their impure motives as detriments to the overall cause, Paul assumes that God is somehow using them for his purposes. He has learned to walk by faith, to see with spiritual eyes what natural eyes cannot see.

God is still working through deeply flawed people. He is not hindered by human insecurities, even when they manifest as egos vying for his stamp of approval. All his true servants, even those with selfish ambitions, are people in process, and God will surely complete what he has begun in them too.

That's important to remember in a world full of egos and insecurities. Through it all, the Kingdom advances not by the perfection of God's people but through their faith.

RE-ENVISION ADVERSARIES

We live in an adversarial society—seemingly heightened by the platforms technology offers—where every interaction seems to have become some sort of critique or assertion of competing interests. Paul's vision is the antidote.

Refuse to be sucked into petty competition. Make it a point to pray for God to work in the lives of your rivals and adversaries. What is he accomplishing through them? How might he be setting them up for an encounter with him? As harmful as their motives or actions might seem, how might God be leveraging them for good? These are not hypothetical questions or idealized hopes. They are acknowledgments of how God often works—and the reason we can rejoice like Paul.

PHILIPPIANS 1:19-26

ULTIMATE ENDS

Beyond his current activities and those of others who were preaching the gospel (or something like it), the crux of Paul's situation was the impending resolution of his court case. How would it turn out? The Philippians were surely wondering with concern, and Paul had no news to tell them that might relieve those concerns—except, of course, that he was completely unconcerned himself. What appeared to be a monumental crisis was for Paul a win-win situation. He assured his readers that however it turned out—even if it ended in death—God's ultimate purposes would be served.

BACKGROUND

Paul's offenses typically would not have been considered capital crimes from a Roman perspective—most officials would think of them as an internal religious matter—and may have been nearing a statute of limitations (possibly two years after appealing to Caesar). Still, his situation was filled with uncertainty. He could be released, but he could also be executed. One never knew with unpredictable emperors and their desire to keep the peace at the expense of personal rights. But as far as Paul was concerned, either outcome had its benefits.

THE BIG PICTURE

Throughout Philippians 1, Paul has been talking about himself, but he never highlights himself as the main character in this story. This is first and foremost about Jesus and the gospel, and within that overarching story, it is about Paul's fruitfulness and the benefits the Philippians might gain from it. Paul has made it clear up to this point that this letter is not a narrative of his personal agenda.

That's a perspective he wants the Philippian believers to embrace, as he makes clear in subsequent passages. We are not the main character in our personal stories either. The whole point of any believer's life is to magnify Christ, to further his purposes, to let his Spirit work through us, and to leverage whatever we have in this world for the growth of God's Kingdom. Personal agendas, including those related to living and dying, give way to such a magnificent vision. Our entire lives are given to a greater purpose—and become all the greater for it.

COMPLETELY AT PEACE

I know that as you pray for me and the Spirit of Jesus Christ helps me, this will lead to my deliverance.

1:19

Later in this letter, Paul will urge his readers not to be anxious about anything but instead to make their requests to God with gratitude. Then God's peace will guard their hearts and minds (4:6-7). Before he gets there, though, Paul shows them what that looks like. "I know . . . this will lead to my deliverance," he tells them. The Philippians have prayed, and Paul is at peace. He is confident that their prayers will be heard and answered.

This is the second time Paul refers to prayer in the context of joy and gratitude and then expresses confidence that God will answer. Grateful for the Philippians' friendship and support, he makes requests on their behalf "with joy" and is "certain" that God will continue his work in them (1:3-6). Combining requests with gratitude and joy, which leads to confidence and peace, seems to be a pattern for Paul in more ways than one—exemplifying what he teaches in personal practice. He seems to have had no doubt that prayers originating in that emotional environment—joy, gratitude, then peace—were invariably answered by God.

If anyone had a right to be unsettled by his circumstances, Paul did. He had been in various forms of confinement for at least two years, probably longer, and the outcome (from a human perspective) was still uncertain. As he went on to explain, he could live or die. Most people in that situation would be a bundle of nerves. Paul seemed completely at rest.

What was the difference? Most people would see potential execution as the undoing of their vision—the loss of a dream, the end of their plans, the unraveling of everything they had hoped for. But Paul's dream was a life of fruitfulness and an eternity with Christ. He knew death would come at some point; when that might be was a detail that had little effect on his goals. Whether he lived or died in the coming weeks, months, or years, he would end up with a life of fruitfulness and an eternity with Christ. Nothing about the situation threatened his ultimate vision.

RE-ENVISION YOUR PURPOSE

Most of us have desires and plans for our lives that we've added to the big picture of being fruitful and spending eternity in heaven. There's nothing wrong with that; God isn't opposed to smaller visions and sometimes puts those desires and plans in our hearts. But when those smaller pictures become our big picture while fruitfulness and eternity become secondary, we easily lose our peace when our ideas are threatened. Then death does unravel our vision. It's the end of what we hoped for.

Surprisingly, letting go of our plans can increase our confidence that God will fulfill them. As Paul demonstrates in the next few verses, he will be fine if the Philippians' prayers do not lead to his deliverance. But because he isn't overly attached to a specific outcome, he can envision the outcome that would be best. Relinquishing our smaller visions to God in favor of the ultimate vision of fruitfulness and eternal fellowship with him has a way of clarifying those smaller visions. We can trust God with them. And our hearts can be at peace.

LIVING WITHOUT COMPROMISE

I fully expect and hope that I will never be ashamed, but that I will continue to be bold for Christ, as I have been in the past.

1:20

It's human nature to try to get the most out of life. We want to maximize our pleasure and minimize our pain. It's also human nature, based on the divine imprint we were given at Creation, to want our lives to be filled with meaning and purpose and to have lasting impact. What happens when those two desires come against each other? How do we respond when our pleasure/pain impulses are at odds with our meaning/purpose impulses? We may have to compromise one or the other.

Paul was aware of the possibility of compromise, and he expected never to be ashamed by his choices. He was not referring to an inward emotional shame but an outward response of shame (see also Romans 1:16). In Greek and Roman cultures, shame and honor were social currency. A person lived either honorably or in disgrace (or sometimes alternated between them), not only in critical moments when all eyes were watching but also in day-to-day behavior and relationships. An honorable life was made up of a multitude of decisions. For Paul, honor implied boldness for Christ, and he had consistently chosen to be bold in the past. Now with the threat of pain and death, he had resolved to maintain his testimony and honor his Lord, regardless of the costs. There would be no compromise here.

Paul was physically in a precarious position. The empire had control over his body, and his life was in its hands. But contrary to the declarations of imperial loyalists, Caesar was not his lord. Jesus was. No matter how much power the empire seemed to have, Paul had a choice in how he lived and, one way or another, would continue to offer himself to Jesus. Whether in life or death—or actually in both—Paul would glorify Christ.

RE-ENVISION YOUR CHOICES

We live in a precarious position too—usually not in a life-or-death situation, but still under constant pressure from our culture to either conform to its image or experience the discomfort of noncompliance. We daily make choices about honor and shame. Will we honor Jesus and therefore risk being shamed by our world? Or will we honor our world and risk dishonoring Christ? When our pleasure/pain impulses are at odds with our meaning/purpose impulses, which will we value more? These are not rare choices to make. They confront us in subtle ways every day.

When you see your life as a series of choices to honor Christ, everything takes on a new meaning. There are a lot of ways to honor Jesus, including enjoying his many gifts and blessings. A lifestyle of honor does not mean living under legalistic pressure to avoid offending him, as though he quenches all desires and restricts our pleasures. The abundant life he offers comes with freedom and joy. But it does mean living without compromise. We abandon ourselves to him, boldly worship him, and see ourselves as instruments of his glory in life and death. We are his, and he is ours. And in his eyes, we will never be ashamed.

A WIN-WIN SITUATION

I trust that my life will bring honor to Christ, whether I live or die. For to me, living means living for Christ, and dying is even better. But if I live, I can do more fruitful work for Christ. So I really don't know which is better.

1:20-22

Picture yourself as a farmer who has been given an almost magical opportunity. The seeds you plant in this season, before the winds shift and the rains come, will not only produce a bountiful harvest. The harvest will remain continually plentiful and will even multiply forever. If you plant just a few rows, you'll enjoy the crops from those rows without end. If you plant many rows, you'll enjoy an even greater abundance. It's up to you, but the time to plant is limited to this season. Once that window closes, there's nothing you can do to add to your work and increase this harvest.

Given that opportunity, most people would press on while they can—even if they're already weary and ready for a rest. Rest can come later; planting can't. It's important to maximize the possibilities of the moment.

Paul is in a situation like this as he looks toward his future ministry, however long it happens to last. At this point in his life, he has been beaten and abused many times, and even though God heals and strengthens, Paul is likely bone-weary and looking forward to eternity with Jesus. He writes as though he has a choice—to remain or die—and perhaps he does, whether by praying for one or the other or answering the authorities a certain way. But in either case, it's a win. As with every other situation in this chapter, he can't lose. Either he continues to bear eternal fruit while the window is open, or even better, he gets to be with Christ in a place of joyful rest.

Not everyone views the end of life so optimistically, even when they have believed in Christ for their salvation. Many miss the opportunity to continue planting, dread their years of "decline," or underestimate the glories to come. Rather than being consumed with a vision of fruitfulness-then-fulfillment, many anticipate instead a path of fading-and-finality. In place of a win-win, we brace for the anticlimax.

Paul had it right. God is setting us up for a magnificent harvest and celebration. Even in our waning years, when we no longer work like we used to, we can continue demonstrating the love of the Father and planting seeds of the Kingdom through prayers of intercession for this world before the throne of the universe. And when the season of planting ends, the rest for weary souls is . . . well, heavenly. It's worthy of our deepest desires and "far better" than we can imagine (see 1:23).

RE-ENVISION YOUR LIFE AND DEATH

Do you see life as a series of experiences to be had and death as "the great unknown"? If so, you'll probably live with a focus on making the best of today (and perhaps the next few decades) and hope that heaven, while probably wonderful, is still a long way off. But if you see life as a once-in-eternity opportunity to bear everlasting fruit, knowing that you'll enjoy that fruit and a spectacularly fulfilling relationship with Christ in heaven forever, you'll find it much easier to make sacrifices now, even as you look forward to your ultimate destiny. Like Paul, you'll be torn between desires for now and desires for later—a glorious place to be.

THE WEIGHT OF ETERNITY

I'm torn between two desires: I long to go and be with Christ, which would be far better for me. But for your sakes, it is better that I continue to live.

1:23-24

Paul seems to think he has a choice. He could go be with Christ or remain in the flesh for the sake of the Philippians and other believers. Being with Christ would be better, for obvious reasons; leaving behind a beaten body and living in heaven is our ultimate fulfillment, the glory that far outweighs our momentary troubles (Romans 8:18; 2 Corinthians 4:17). But we can leverage earthly opportunities for Kingdom fruitfulness only while we're here, which can only enhance future glory. Paul writes as though he is choosing between these two desires, even though the outcome of his trial seems to be in imperial hands.

Is this a statement of faith that whatever he chooses to pray for will happen? If so, this is a transforming picture of prayer—God giving his servants a choice in some either-or contingency in his purposes. Or is Paul simply picking which option to root for, knowing that it is out of his hands—even though he has already expressed confidence in his deliverance (Philippians 1:19) and will do so again in the next few words (1:25)? Either way, he is demonstrating the intersection between God's will and ours, and it isn't nearly so rigidly defined as we might imagine. Paul's journey is known to God but is still open-ended, at least from an earthly perspective. And either way, it would work out well.

We can't have that perspective if we cling to our own agendas. If our goal is to have a nice, convenient, comfortable life, we'll find our circumstances working at cross-purposes with that goal much of the time. But if our goal is to glorify Jesus, behold him, serve him, and ultimately be with him, circumstances can't thwart us. We will always have an opportunity to do that regardless of what we face. Circumstances actually serve those purposes one way or another.

RE-ENVISION YOUR VULNERABILITY

If you see yourself as a victim of circumstances, vulnerable to the forces at work around you, tossed around by the waves of an unpredictable life, threatened by contradictions to your dreams and desires, you aren't alone. You come from a long line of people struggling under the vagaries of human existence. But if you want to come out from under it all, to stand impervious to circumstantial demands, and to become invulnerable even to your own mortality, you can. It's a matter of where you envision the weight of your life.

A predominantly present-weighted life is preoccupied with a vision of here-and-now experiences, which, though important, are actually only a small picture of God's purposes for us. An eternity-weighted life is preoccupied with eternal fruitfulness—advancing the Kingdom in this age while anticipating its fullness forever. Where we place our vision determines how vulnerable we feel. A perspective that focuses on the eternal reorients our desires, magnifies our hopes, minimizes our fears, and leads us into eternity with confidence.

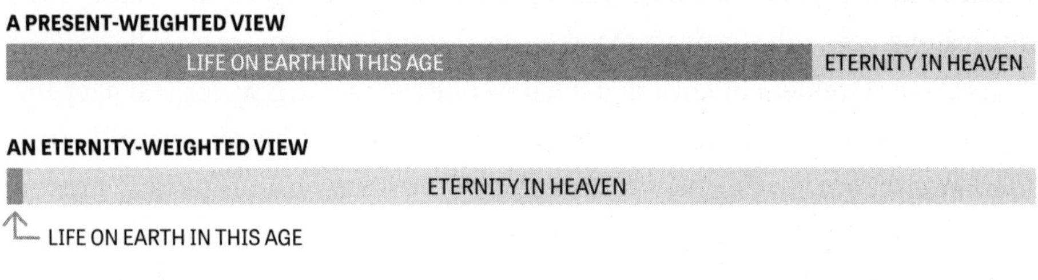

A weighted perspective: With a present-weighted view of life, we focus most of our thoughts and energy on our here-and-now experiences, perhaps valuing eternity but not orienting everything in our lives around it. With an eternity-weighted view, we still value life in the here and now and plan accordingly, but we consider everything in light of eternal experience and fruitfulness. This shapes all our hopes, fears, desires, plans, relationships, and much more.

NO LIMITATIONS

Knowing this, I am convinced that I will remain alive so I can continue to help all of you grow and experience the joy of your faith. And when I come to you again, you will have even more reason to take pride in Christ Jesus because of what he is doing through me.

1:25-26

At no point has Paul seemed outraged or put out by his situation and the injustice of it. In fact, in many ways he asked for it. His appeal to Caesar (Acts 25:11-12) probably wasn't necessary (see Acts 26:32), but it did give him a free ride into Rome and its power structures. For Paul, everything was an opportunity, not a setback. Even his "setbacks" furthered his mission.

This attitude was possible because he saw the mission as the priority. Everything he experienced on earth could be leveraged either to advance the Kingdom or demonstrate it. If people were growing into the image of Christ through his ministry, whether through initial salvation or ongoing spiritual maturity, the Kingdom was expanding on earth. If Paul was being thwarted in his effort to win and develop new believers, the adversity gave him a stage to display Kingdom attitudes and perspectives, laying the groundwork for Kingdom expansion through that testimony. No matter what happened, the Kingdom within him and beyond him could not be suppressed. Every attempt to stamp it out would strengthen it—at least as long as he maintained the right perspective.

The critical component of that perspective was Christ working in him. This work was not just the mission of Paul; it was the mission of Jesus. It was the love of Christ that compelled him (2 Corinthians 5:14, NIV). He was driven by the greatness of God's power given to those who believe (Ephesians 1:19-20), strengthened by the God who can accomplish more than anything we ask or think according to the power operating within us (Ephesians 3:20), filled with the hope of glory dwelling within (Colossians 1:27). Or, as Paul would soon remind the Philippians, God was shaping them both to desire and to accomplish his purposes (Philippians 2:13). In other words, this was no human endeavor. It was divinely orchestrated, empowered, and fulfilled.

RE-ENVISION SETBACKS

If Jesus is at work within you—not just to transform you but also to drive you forward in your purpose—then every situation is an occasion for him to work. Jesus is never being thwarted by your circumstances; he is using them to advance his Kingdom. He is never limited by the people around you; his Spirit is irrepressible in those who continue to rest in him. Even your own mistakes are no obstacle; God has a long history of working through flawed people and incorporating their flaws into his plans, as the Bible repeatedly and resoundingly testifies. Like Paul, you can look at everything in your past and present as Kingdom collateral. One way or another, it can serve God's purposes—and, if your vision is aligned with his, your purposes too.

This perspective is hard to maintain unless you've caught a vision of the irrepressible God who never throws his hands up in resignation over anything in your life. No matter how much you regret a situation or decision, it's material for him to work with. The Christ who is living within you is not frustrated by your limitations. He leverages them—and all your experiences—for his Kingdom. In everything you encounter, let him.

PHILIPPIANS 1:27-30

A NEW WAY OF LIFE

This passage is a transition from everything Paul has been talking about to everything to come. He has shown them how he has been living in a manner worthy of the gospel. He has displayed Kingdom attitudes and perspectives in every situation he has faced. Now he urges the Philippians to do the same. His role-modeling leads to application, and now that they have seen what a worthy lifestyle looks like, they can live it out. Their vision precedes their action.

Without saying so directly, Paul has made his point: "You see the enormity of my problems—and how small they seem to me? Now how big do your problems seem to you?" Of course, he is much gentler with them than that, and his perspective has broader implications. These believers are not merely to adopt a new perspective; they are to adopt a lifestyle in their fellowship that represents the gospel well. They aren't just messengers of the Good News; they are to be demonstrations of it.

BACKGROUND

Paul provides his first allusion to citizenship—a theme of the letter—but does not give a comprehensive look at what citizenship entails (this passage uses a Greek word that only hints at it), but he outlines some of the duties associated with living out one's political, communal responsibilities. But which polity? Which community? Certainly not that of Rome or Philippi, at least as a primary focus. These believers were grounded in another realm with altogether different loyalties. And those loyalties would at times conflict with those of the city and the empire.

We don't know what kind of suffering and enemies Paul was referring to when he turned his focus to the Philippians' relationship with their city, but severe persecution seems unlikely. There's no reference to physical danger or imprisonment in this letter, and the church had money to send him, so they seem to have been doing pretty well. Paul mentions only vague threats: social (intimidating enemies), internal (discord), and doctrinal (legalism). But social marginalization could be a real threat in this proudly Roman colony, where "eastern" religions were looked down upon. Paul discovered that bias on his first visit to the city as local businessmen directed an inflated accusation at Paul and his companions: "These Jews" were creating an uproar by "teaching customs that are illegal for us Romans to practice" (Acts 16:20-21). Non-Roman influences were not particularly welcome there.

THE BIG PICTURE

Whatever they were facing, the Philippian believers perceived it as adversity and were apparently daunted by it. Paul's rhetorical strategy was to put things in perspective and demonstrate just how minimal their adversity was in light of the promises, power, fellowship, and joy they had been given. His big vision made their preoccupations look small.

Part of that vision was the opportunity to display the nature of the Kingdom in a non-Kingdom culture. Non-Christian Philippians may have been making life uncomfortable for this church, but its mission was not about comfort. It was to demonstrate redemption and life in Christ and how the Holy Spirit changes hearts, minds, and relationships. The believers were to look beyond themselves—and their sufferings—to advance the Kingdom where they were.

ABOVE ALL

Above all, you must live as citizens of heaven.

1:27

Paul knew a thing or two about citizenship. His status as a Roman citizen served him well on several occasions, and many of his readers would likely recall the magistrates' unfortunate neglect of his status on his first visit to the city (Acts 16:37-39). Now he reminds the Philippians of their true identity. Perhaps they've been acting as if they are merely citizens of Rome or residents of Philippi, or even just citizens of earth. If so, they've been caught up in the small picture instead of the grand vision.

Paul has spent much of the first part of his letter reorienting their view, demonstrating how radically a redeemed and faith-filled perspective can reveal the Kingdom at work behind the scenes.

- "You're having some problems with each other? Don't worry; God will keep growing you toward full maturity."
- "You're concerned about my imprisonment? If you could only see what God is doing through it!"
- "Self-centered preachers are trying to make a name for themselves? Okay, but they're still publicizing the name of Christ, and more people are hearing about him."

- "You're concerned for my life? Yes, I might die. But you know what? Either way, I win!"

The apostle who appeared to be near the end of his ministry and stuck in a place of fruitlessness pulled back the curtain to unveil the plot behind the plot, and it was magnificent. By Kingdom criteria, nothing was as it appeared. God's work was flourishing.

That's the lens to look through, and Paul here turns toward the readers and hearers of his letter as if to say, "Now take everything I've been saying about my circumstances and apply it to yours." The implications are monumental: With this vision, they would conduct themselves in a manner worthy of the gospel, stand together in unity of purpose, become fearless in the face of their enemies, and endure their suffering well. A proper vision is more than just an encouraging view. It changes everything.

That's why Paul positions it as a singular focus—"above all." This focus is a priority because it's powerful. It aligns us with the heart and vision of God.

RE-ENVISION YOUR CITIZENSHIP

Most Christians live with an earth-to-heaven orientation. We're on earth trying to pull down the blessings of heaven through prayer, faith, and service. We see ourselves as lacking heaven's resources, so we plead with God to give them to us.

But what if we're already seated with Christ in heavenly places (Ephesians 2:6)? What if we've already been raised with Christ and our life is wrapped up in him, where he is (Colossians 3:1-4)? What if the difference between answered and unanswered prayer is a matter of recognizing what we've already been given and believing it, or experiencing the Kingdom is a matter of uprooting ourselves from a worldly point of view? What if it's entirely legitimate to live with a heaven-to-earth orientation even while we're on earth?

Seeing yourself as a citizen of heaven—a thought further developed later in the letter (especially Philippians 3:20)—comes with a multitude of implications: unshakable faith, fearlessness, a clearer vision of God's Kingdom and your place in it, rightly ordered priorities, eternal values, a spirit of endurance, and deep roots in the love of God, to name a few. The issue is not striving for what you want to receive; it's believing what you've already been granted. And it begins with changing the way you see.

AS ONE

. . . standing together with one spirit and one purpose . . .

1:27

People who have grown up in a competitive environment tend to view other human beings as competitors. Those who have experienced rejection tend to live like they have something to prove to everyone else. Many who have been taught that they are valuable primarily for what they can accomplish are driven by a need to perform and achieve. These and other impulses, shaped so subtly and deeply by our upbringing and environment, color our view of other human beings. Our fundamental insecurities shape our relationships. We tend to see people through the distorted lenses of our own drives and desires.

Unfortunately, these lenses carry over into our lives as believers if we don't apply the gospel to them. Salvation by grace through faith doesn't automatically change how we see everyone—unless we've had a radically reorienting vision of our new identity. If we aren't careful, we may look to other believers for the validation only God can give. Or we may see them as competitors to our calling. Either way, we mentally categorize them as useful or not—as either an obstacle or a means to an end—and then grow discouraged or offended when they don't fit our purposes. They become mere players on the stage of our lives.

In truth, other believers are foundational to our calling—God has designed his people for interdependence—so we can't fulfill our purpose if we don't see them from a God-given perspective. We need the gifts other people offer, and they need ours. We also can't impact our culture effectively without other believers. The world's view of Christianity is shaped by its view of Christians collectively, whether we like it or not. As much as we like to think in terms of "my" testimony, real influence comes when the testimony is "ours." Or, as Jesus put it, they will know *us* by *our* love (John 13:35).

This was apparently an issue with the Philippians. Paul mentions agreement, unity, and partnership (or their contradictions) again and again in this letter (Philippians 1:5, 15-16, 27, 30; 2:1-4, 21; 3:15; 4:2-3), and he directly relates believers' harmony to their impact on the society around them (1:27-28; 2:14-16; 4:5). How well they got along with each other affected their experience of God and how they influenced their world.

RE-ENVISION YOUR FELLOWSHIP

How do you see other believers? Are they bystanders to your calling or essential to fulfilling it? Competitors or teammates? Individual members or part of the body? Your answers to those questions carry more weight than you might think. Your purpose and theirs are inextricably tied together. Your impact on society depends on them.

That alone ought to cause believers to zealously and relentlessly pursue unity of spirit and purpose. This does not mean we all need to agree on everything or behave uniformly. It does mean we need to live in harmony with each other, blow wind in each other's sails, and trust that our different gifts and perspectives all serve a purpose in the Kingdom. It takes many kinds of expression to demonstrate the heart of God in this world. But the heart must beat as one.

AN ILLUSION OF DEFEAT

. . . fighting together for the faith.

1:27

Imagine an army returning from the battlefield with downcast eyes and heavy legs, its soldiers straggling out of formation with no sense of decorum or comradery. You overhear critiques of each other's performance at the battlefront and suspicions of those in charge.

How bad did they lose? you wonder, only to find out they didn't. In fact, the battle isn't even over. They saw the threat, decided the enemy had momentum and a tactical advantage, and just gave up and came home. They never noticed the multitudes fighting with them or figured out how to use the extraordinarily powerful weapons they had been given.

That's a picture of some believers in trying times. They have relied on their natural eyes and astonishingly decided the eyes of faith must have deceived them. They read today's headlines, lament a lost culture, and drag their wounded morale home—often casting shade on each other's efforts. Like Saul's army staring at the size of Goliath, describing his formidable weapons in excruciating detail, and listening to his intimidating threats as though they actually meant something (1 Samuel 17:4-11), they have forgotten that they serve the armies of the living God (1 Samuel 17:26). They've broken ranks and surrendered in the battle they were promised to win—before it's even over.

Too dramatic? Maybe. But listen to the conversations many people of "faith" have about the times we are living in. They hardly instill hope, even though we are filled with the Spirit of "the source of hope" (Romans 15:13). Those conversations often neglect the fact that God has defended his people throughout history and drawn billions into saving faith. They somehow ignore the stories of God dramatically turning the tables in Exodus, Ruth, Esther, numerous psalms, and a tomb in Jerusalem. And they reflect no vision of the great cloud of witnesses that testify of certain victory, no matter how things look.

We are united not only with that "huge crowd of witnesses" (Hebrews 12:1) but also with armies of faith-filled believers on earth. In fact, that hopeful and victorious fellowship is one of our greatest strengths. Facing adversity is a team sport in God's Kingdom, and when we approach it that way, God makes sport of the adversity sooner or later. He is a master at turning the tide. His people simply need to stand together and face the battle long enough to see the victorious outcome.

RE-ENVISION YOUR VICTORY

Whatever challenges the Philippians faced, they needed to see the truth at their disposal. God filling his people—together—with his presence and power makes for an invincible combination in our defense of the faith. This truth is difficult for those in an individualistic culture to grasp, but it's an important one. Unity of spirit and purpose are high priorities of God for his people and a source of ultimate victory. Petty differences of the kind the Philippians were apparently experiencing (Philippians 4:2) distract from living out the gospel in a society hostile to it and create an illusion of defeat. A vision of who God's people really are eliminates the distraction and breaks the illusion. In any context—including ancient Philippi and our own society—Christians demonstrating oneness in Christ can turn the tide of an entire culture.

NEVER BACK DOWN

Don't be intimidated in any way by your enemies.

1:28

Paul has implied that the Philippians need a clearer vision of each other (1:27). Now he says they need a clearer vision of their enemies. Apparently they are intimidated—an unbefitting attitude for Christians who see the big picture. Afraid of people who don't know the truth, are not aligned with the God of the universe, and cannot look forward to a glorious eternity unless they are radically saved? Why would any believer bow their heart to someone in such a disastrous position? They wouldn't—if they saw that position for what it is.

What Paul is really calling for in this passage is a new view of God, of themselves, and of those who don't know the truth. God is the author of all that is true and the defender of all who trust him. Believers are secure in his will and already rooted in a glorious eternity. Nonbelievers are living in ignorance and sabotaging their own destiny. We should feel enormous compassion for them but never fear them. They know not what they do. We, on the other hand, are well aware of what God is doing and how we've become a part of it. If we're fearful, intimidated, or discouraged, we are looking at people or situations through a distorted lens.

Will there be setbacks? Absolutely. Some of them may even be deadly, as Paul made clear in earlier verses. But all of them are ephemeral, mere illusions and lightweight impostors in the face of eternity. The Kingdom is full of Christians who fear things that cannot ultimately hurt them, who dread defeat in spite of multiple assurances of victory, and who compromise with evil while being called to stand for truth. We've forgotten that in order to win a battle, there actually has to be a battle. Adversity shouldn't be a surprise.

Many Christians think their need for perseverance is a sign of something wrong. Paul says instead that it's a sign of victory. Endurance is a normal part of our calling. We've become citizens of a heavenly Kingdom who still live in a fallen world. But we are destined to outlast that world.

RE-ENVISION YOUR TENACITY

If you see yourself as powerless in the face of adversity, you'll wilt. If you see yourself filled with the resurrected Jesus who can never be defeated, you'll persist. You may even look with amusement at how the conflict plays out, knowing that in time it will be resolved. You never need to wonder if you're on the verge of defeat. By definition as a believer, you aren't. By some eternal measure, whether natural eyes see it or not, faith always wins its victories.

But for faith to win its victories in your life, you'll need to change the way you see. You'll have to anchor yourself in who God says he is, who he says you are, and who he says your adversaries are. Wavering on any component of that visionary package will open doors to fears, doubts, and resignation. Immersing yourself in it builds faith, hope, and resolve. The former posture causes you to shrink back from your enemies. The latter empowers you to love them. And it creates the testimony your world needs to see.

NOW YOU

You have been given . . . the privilege of suffering for him. We are in this struggle together.

1:29-30

The language shifted in 1:27. Paul had been talking about his own experiences ever since his gracious introductory words and his prayer for Philippian believers (1:1-11), but in 1:27 he began talking about "you." His rather revolutionary view of his circumstances was very informative and inspiring, but he didn't present this perspective just so his friends in Philippi would be up to date on his situation. There was a greater purpose in it, and the transition of 1:27-30 spells it out. Paul's attitude toward his confinement, his adversaries, and his uncertain future was more than encouragement. It was an example to follow—or better yet, a vision to embrace.

Paul makes it abundantly clear that he was living in a bigger picture than the Philippians might have seen with their natural eyes. Here, by emphasizing their shared struggles, he demonstrates that they were meant to live in a bigger picture too. A narrow focus might have them preoccupied with their "enemies" (1:28) and their "suffering" (1:29). In fact, if we read between the lines, that's apparently where their vision was directed. They seem to have been living in the here and now, trying to navigate the challenges right in front of them without stepping back and seeing those challenges from heaven's perspective. They needed to open their spiritual eyes.

We don't know what trials they faced, but we do know from Paul's words what heaven's perspective on those trials was. Their enemies presented temporary opposition and were headed toward defeat, but the Philippian believers were already saved and headed toward a glorious future (1:28). And in the grand scheme of things, suffering for Christ was a privilege (1:29). Jesus himself said so (Matthew 5:10-12). Everything that intimidated and threatened them fell into Paul's famous category of "light and momentary" (2 Corinthians 4:17, NIV). Like Paul, whose troubles surely loomed larger than theirs from a human perspective, they needed to stop gazing only at whatever was staring them in the face.

RE-ENVISION YOUR FAITH

Whatever you gaze at gets bigger, at least figuratively if not literally. This is how molehills of problems turn into mountains of despair, how slight possibilities turn into burdensome anxieties, how empty threats turn into full-blown portents of doom. It's also how faith disappears. It's impossible to fill your vision with the bad and still believe in the good.

What's the remedy? Stubbornly refuse negative perspectives—a point Paul will return to in 4:8. Relentlessly fill your mind and heart with gratitude, joy, and hope in all the possibilities of God's Kingdom—a point Paul has demonstrated almost from the first word of the letter. What you look at, spiritually speaking, determines your attitude for the day and the course of your life. Steward that power well. Your experiences of God's Kingdom—and the experiences of those around you—depend on it.

PHILIPPIANS 2:1-11

A PICTURE OF TRUTH AND LOVE

Paul urged the Philippians to live in a manner worthy of the Good News (1:27), then cast a vision for what that would look like in standing together and facing adversity without fear (1:27-30). His next instructions continue that theme, especially on the matter of unity. Creating an environment of Kingdom life involves humility, a sacrificial spirit, genuine fellowship, and a desire to love more than to be right. The fellowship of believers should be marked by affection—in fact, by the affection of Jesus himself, as Paul claimed in 1:8.

For those unfamiliar with life in God's Kingdom, Philippians 2 presents a surprising picture. Paul has already indicated that suffering for Christ is a privilege (1:29). Now he reminds his readers that in God's Kingdom, the way up is to go down. The way to impact the world is not primarily through confrontation but by simply shining (2:15)—living as an embodiment of Christ, the one who gave up his privileges of God-ness, who demonstrated greatness through serving, and who was exalted by lowering himself. If you're going to see yourself as a citizen of heaven, this is what that citizenship often entails.

BACKGROUND

We know from the letter of Philippians that the fellowship was becoming fractured in some way by disagreement. This is apparent in the conflict between Euodia and Syntyche (4:2), as well as in the examples Paul gave—his own attitude toward rival preachers, for instance (1:12-18)—and his frequent instructions to be of one mind. We don't know the nature of these conflicts, whether they were personal, doctrinal, or something else. But Paul seems remarkably unconcerned about establishing correct points of view (unless the core of the gospel is at stake, as in 3:2) and is much more focused on harmonious relationships. Maintaining fellowship in the community is a much higher priority than the differences of its members.

THE BIG PICTURE

Truth is important, of course, but is simply verbal clutter if not saturated in love (1 Corinthians 13:1-3). That's why the example of Jesus is so important. He spoke words of truth but demonstrated love in all of them. In fact, if we (like the Philippians) are to step into the picture Paul paints in these verses, we should begin with a majestic vision of who Jesus is, what he did, the spirit in which he did it, and what it accomplished for him and us. Paul gives us that vision in Philippians 2:6-11, a piece of poetic praise (and perhaps a commonly sung hymn) of Jesus, the servant who rules.

We could try to train ourselves to practice the principles of these verses—that's how many people approach biblical truth—but when the vision is strong, the principles are absorbed and the practices seem to happen naturally. Paul's aim here is to inspire more than inform. Gazing at the sacrificial humility of Jesus is more than sufficient to set the tone of fellowship among his people. When the magnificence of his incarnation, sacrifice, and exaltation fills our eyes, this template he created for us guides our lives.

THE HEART OF THE SPIRIT

Is there any encouragement from belonging to Christ? Any comfort from his love? Any fellowship together in the Spirit? Are your hearts tender and compassionate?

2:1

Paul has already filled this letter with joy. He has claimed the affection of Christ. He has expressed love and warmth, even while challenging his readers to make some adjustments in their lives. He certainly has thoughts on truth—that is eminently clear in all his writings—but in this letter he has majored on attitudes. So his approach to the Philippians' discord shouldn't surprise us. He appeals to the emotions and attitudes of their hearts to guide their minds.

That may seem backward to us, as thoroughly as we've been steeped in the priority of reason. We have been raised and discipled to subordinate our emotions to our knowledge. Facts come first, then feelings. We're supposed to enjoy good emotions when we have them, but we should never be led by them. That's what we've been taught.

Paul envisions a different process, at least in this situation. Just as there is a sorrow that leads to repentance and truth (2 Corinthians 7:9-10), there are affections that lead to unity. He knows these believers have tenderness and compassion for each other, but their disagreements are getting in the way. It is very clear that he does not expect them to settle those disagreements *so* their hearts can be united again. It's the other way around. Their hearts are already bound together; their minds need to catch up.

This is one example of what it means to be led by the Spirit, who is not nearly as unemotional as many assume him to be. Unity in the body of Christ is not about eliminating diverse thought so much as it is about being drawn together in love. While Christians have split fellowship over doctrinal differences for centuries—to the effect of tens of thousands of denominations—the Spirit still wants us to enjoy his company together.

RE-ENVISION YOUR AFFECTIONS

As citizens of heaven (1:27; 3:20), we'll need to get used to that reality. The Kingdom is characterized by joy, laughter, love, celebrations, warm embraces, and hearts overflowing with affection. No image of heaven in Scripture pictures theological debates or personality conflicts. Citizens of heaven who currently live here on earth need to remember our primary culture. If we immerse ourselves in a vision of what heaven looks like, our lives and relationships on earth tend to take on the same nature.

This isn't an appeal to "follow your heart" above all else. Truth matters, and the heart (like the mind) can lead us astray. But don't ignore your heart either. The Spirit works there. Sometimes he works there first. Notice when he does, and build your relationships on the bonds of fellowship he is strengthening.

WHOLEHEARTED AGREEMENT

Make me truly happy by agreeing wholeheartedly with each other, loving one another, and working together with one mind and purpose.

2:2

Jesus prayed that his followers would be one just as he and the Father are one (John 17:20-21). That's an astonishing prayer—the Father and Son are closer than we can imagine—but Jesus would not have prayed it if it were not possible. Unity is God's desire for his people.

Many would look at Christianity today and lament how far short we have fallen of this ideal. After all, many are barely able to go to church with people they disagree with on matters of theological, social, or political significance. Church history is filled with disputes and schisms. We are hardly known for unity. And society as a whole, including Christians, seems to be trending toward increasing isolation.

So does all that mean we don't have unity? Not really. Despite appearances, God has bound his people together as one. We are born of one Spirit, children of one Father, citizens of one heaven, and filled with one ultimate hope. We may not recognize the unity we have, but God nevertheless sees all of us as being in Christ. The question isn't whether we're one. It's whether we'll live up to the oneness we have.

RE-ENVISION YOUR PEOPLE

As with most truths in the Christian life, living out our unity is a matter of what we choose to see. Do we relate to other believers with the assumption that unity in the body of Christ is already a fact, a Kingdom reality we simply need to step into? Or do we relate to other believers with the assumption that we don't yet have unity and need to strive for it? One will lead to perpetual frustration—a pursuit of full agreement, wholehearted affection, or some other ideal that never quite comes—while the other changes the way we interact with people right now.

Many in the church prioritize truth over love. Both are vital, but balancing them well involves a specific order. The approach "If we agree, I'll love you" is not the way of the Kingdom. Relationships in Christ take the opposite approach: "Since I love you, let's try to find a way to agree." That might include agreeing to disagree, but doing so in love. This kind of unity is what Paul advocates here.

Having a conversation with someone in order to make a connection with them is rather different from having a conversation when you assume the connection is already there. Or, to put it another way, the dynamics change when you start talking to people as "one of us" rather than "one of them." Who you envision "your people" to be makes all the difference.

When you see another believer as "one of us," you'll find that love, agreement, connection, and unity come much more easily—perhaps not on every issue, but at least in every intent. Hearts and minds that want to bond generally do. And Jesus' prayer continues to be answered.

BE HUMBLE

Don't be selfish; don't try to impress others. Be humble.

2:3

Philippi was steeped in the ways of Rome. It had long been culturally Greek, but as a colony of Rome since the time of Augustus, and with significant numbers of retired Roman soldiers, it had taken on much of the character of the imperial center. Most of its residents embraced Roman ideals and lived according to Roman values. And those values did not put much stock in humility.

To most Romans, humility was a sign of weakness. Couching one's own achievements in the language of humility was acceptable—Augustus himself had done so rather transparently—but winning people's respect and admiration was still the goal. Paul's advice not to impress others ran contrary to the Roman psyche, and to the Greek one too. The people of Philippi would not have been impressed with Paul's ideas.

Minds and hearts steeped in one culture are hard to retrain in another, yet that's what discipleship is all about. Gentile Philippian believers were learning to think in Kingdom ways, which often meant no longer thinking in Roman or Greek ways (and not adopting elements of Jewish culture that ran contrary to the Kingdom). They were stepping into a new, countercultural paradigm. They needed a whole new vision of what human character was supposed to look like.

RE-ENVISION YOUR STATUS

We need this new vision too. The Kingdom is radically countercultural. It also goes against the instincts of fallen human nature. Roman emphases on pride and achievement made sense for those who viewed the world as a competitive arena, where the only goal is to ascend in social status as high as possible. But in the Kingdom, ascent happens in an entirely different way. Fallen human impulses only get in the way. The drive to lift oneself up and impress others leads only to hollow victories.

Humility is not a sign of weakness, nor is it an acknowledgment of unworthiness. In Christ, we have been made both worthy and strong. But humility does reflect an awareness that others have been made worthy and strong too. The insecure are threatened by that fact. Those who see and know who they are in Christ are not.

That points to a fascinating irony: Those who build themselves up with pride actually do so from weakness and insecurity. They need to see themselves through the eyes of others. Believers who have no need to build themselves up with pride rise up from a position of strength. They see themselves and others through the eyes of God, as he defines them. Pride and selfishness lead to fractured relationships and a weakened fellowship. True humility strengthens all who come within its reach—including the one who has it.

A TREASURED IMAGE

. . . thinking of others as better than yourselves.

2:3

Try an experiment. Throughout the day, imagine having created everyone you see. Think of how you might have put unique gifts and characteristics in each person, how much time you might have spent coming up with diverse, innovative personalities to write into each person's DNA, what dreams, desires, and experiences you might have for them, and how eagerly you might watch to see their lives unfold. While they may not be living up to your ideals, you put a lot of effort into designing their potential and planning for them to reach it. Your love and creativity infuse every aspect of your work, and you take great pleasure in watching your people move toward their purpose and grieve every time they move away from it. Most of all, you want them to know how careful and intentional you were with each of them, and, if they're willing, you want them to get to know you better.

That would radically reorient your perception of other people, wouldn't it? It also fits Paul's instructions elsewhere to stop evaluating others from a human point of view (2 Corinthians 5:16). We don't normally look at people that way because we know we aren't God and are clouded by our limited vision. But God invites us to share his heart and see through his eyes, which means seeing people with his love and compassion, longing for them with his desires and affections (Philippians 1:8), and covering them with his grace. When we begin to feel his heartbeat for other people, we begin to feel their heartbeat too.

In the Kingdom, strong relationships and the bonds of unity depend on such a vision. We have to learn to see in new ways and from radically different perspectives. This involves putting ourselves in the place of others, thinking in terms of our new citizenship, and praying with awareness that we are in Christ, already seated in the heavenly realm (see Ephesians 2:6). It means replacing the upside-down values of this world with the right-side-up values of the Kingdom, no matter how disorienting it all may feel at first. When we came to Christ in faith, we entered a new reality. Our view of God, ourselves, others, and our world should reflect it.

RE-ENVISION YOUR RELATIONSHIPS

Few people experience the pleasure of living in a community of deferential, unassuming, mutually affirming, servant-hearted people, but this is what Kingdom communities are supposed to look like. The good news is that we don't have to desperately search for such a community or just wait for one to happen. We can help create this kind of fellowship. Other members may not pick up on the cues at first, and some may take time to embrace the new culture. But the Spirit is keenly interested in cultivating these kinds of fellowship and is there to help. We can ask him to do so. We can look for the ways he is working and partner with him in the process. Our fellowship, and our vision of the people in it, will begin to reflect his nature, and his presence and power will begin to flow through us all.

ALL IN ONE

Don't look out only for your own interests, but take an interest in others, too.

2:4

We are naturally self-interested. That doesn't mean we're all selfish, only that we generally focus on the responsibilities and purposes that fall under our domain. We tend to our own spheres of influence. We don't work hard at our jobs so we can put food on the table for the neighbors' kids. We do it for our kids. We choose our education not to advance someone else's career but to advance our own. We approach life with a limited focus because we can't focus on everything, and the personal desires, dreams, goals, purposes, and needs that have filled our hearts also preoccupy our minds. The world may call this "looking out for number one," but we have to look out for something, and that something is generally whatever is right in front of us.

This is normal even for Kingdom citizens—we each have our own areas of responsibility—but we're also created and called to merge our own interests with those of others. God designed his people to lift their eyes beyond their own agendas and recognize how all Kingdom purposes fit together. We were not created to be independent; the body of Christ depends on each of its members (1 Corinthians 12). That's why no one has every spiritual gift. God has rigged the fellowship so that we need what he has given others and so others need what he has given us. We can't experience everything he wants to give us apart from them; his voice, his gifts, his encouragement, his provision, and much more comes through his people to the benefit of others.

That's why looking out for our own interests to the exclusion of others does not fit the Kingdom culture. Even (or especially) within the Trinity, fellowship is highly valued. In a Kingdom in which every member seeks to serve all others, no one ever has unfulfilled needs. We were created to live and function together.

RE-ENVISION THE BODY

When members of the body of Christ envision themselves as disparate members, the fellowship becomes prone to rivalries and conflicts. People find themselves competing for the same positions, seeking favor from certain leaders or other members, making decisions that benefit themselves over the body as a whole, and more. But if you see the body of Christ as a united whole, every member connected to you as one, you have a much greater stake in the harmony of the fellowship. Other people's well-being affects yours, and yours affects theirs. Everyone becomes keenly interested in every other part of the body because each person's welfare is tied to everyone else's. The body rises or falls, advances or stagnates, grows and matures together.

This vision will radically transform a church, even one that doesn't live up to it perfectly. The fellowship becomes something like heaven and serves as a confounding testimony to the world. Yes, it will involve some sacrifices—Paul will illustrate that in the next few verses—but the rewards are far greater than the costs. The body that envisions itself as one lives as one, and everyone in it is blessed.

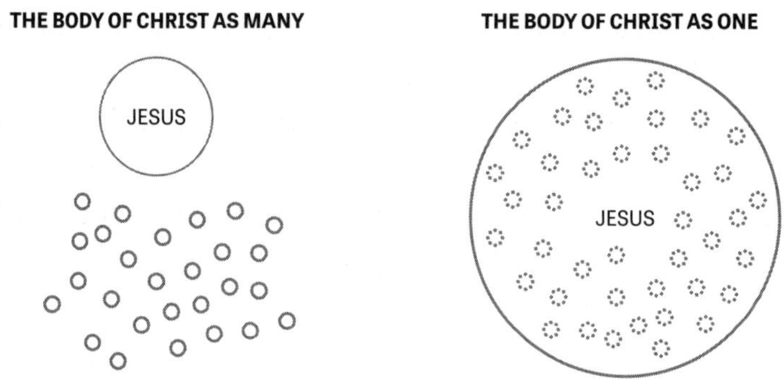

Envisioning the whole: When we see ourselves and other believers as distinct entities with disparate interests, motives, and purposes, we tend to individualize and compete. When we see each other as members of the same body, we're much more likely to look out for the welfare of others. Their well-being is connected to ours, and the body can flourish as one.

BEHOLDING AND BECOMING

You must have the same attitude that Christ Jesus had.

2:5

Young athletes play out the scene every weekend on fields around the world. They adopt the mannerisms, techniques, and swagger of their heroes. They learn to run, throw, kick, catch, jump, and even talk just like the players they idolize, not only because they want to follow in the same path but also simply because they've watched them so many times. They have filled their gaze with a template, and without even trying, they grow toward that vision.

Adults do the same thing, only much more subtly (sometimes) and with a bit more discernment. But we still tend to grow in the direction of whatever we love and admire, and that growth tends to be organic rather than the product of self-imposed discipline. When we're following instructions and principles, we have to train ourselves in new habits and practices. But when we're following a role model who has captured our imagination, change just seems to happen. We always move toward our vision.

After urging the Philippians to embrace humility and live selflessly with one another, Paul turns their attention to a divine role model, a captivating vision of what humility really looks like. He wants them not to just follow instructions but to be inspired. If they would simply fill their hearts and minds with the image of Jesus and let their love for him increase, they would grow into that image and live out his kind of humility. It would radically change the way they related to each other—and the way they influenced the world around them.

RE-ENVISION YOUR TEMPLATE

If you really want to fill your vision with something revolutionary, gaze at Jesus. In the verses that follow, Paul will unfold the trajectory of Jesus' incarnation and exaltation, but it begins with a choice of focus. Savor the imagery of a God who clothes himself in flesh in the humblest circumstances, who, in a peripheral province of a far-reaching empire, against all human odds, changes the world forever, draws humanity back into its original design, and prepares us for an unfathomably glorious eternity. Marvel at how counterintuitively—and even offensively—his humility accomplished the opposite of what anyone might have expected. Celebrate the promise, presence, and power of the God of the universe who even now is filling his people with his Spirit. Jesus is a hero worth loving. And that love will thoroughly transform your life.

THE DIVINE TRAJECTORY

Though he was God, . . . he gave up his divine privileges, . . . was born as a human being, . . . and died a criminal's death on a cross. Therefore, God elevated him to the place of highest honor and gave him the name above all other names.

2:6-9

In a remarkable demonstration of his divine descent into servanthood, Jesus took off his robe, wrapped a slave's towel around his waist, washed his disciples' feet, put his robe back on, and began to teach about a very painful present and a very promising future (John 13:18–16:33). At the time, his followers could not have understood the full implications of this display, but in light of his life, ministry, death, resurrection, and ascension, it all makes sense. God clothed himself in humanity, served us in order to teach and redeem and restore us, sacrificed himself to deal with the consequences of human rebellion, conquered death, and is now exalted forever. To say it was the most shocking story in the history of the universe still seems to be something of an understatement.

This trajectory of descending into extreme depths to ascend into ultimate heights looks upside down to human eyes. Going down to go up doesn't make sense to us. Like many paradoxes of the Kingdom—becoming a servant to be great, giving as a condition for receiving, losing our lives in order to save them, perfecting our strength through weakness, dying in order to live—humility as the pathway to exaltation seems absurd. But this is the trail Jesus blazed, and though he is certainly exceptional, he lived this trajectory as an example for us. We are lifted up by willingly choosing to go down.

It's the world's way that is upside down, of course, and the Kingdom's way that is right side up. Paul has already exemplified this trajectory in several circumstances (Philippians 1), and he will continue to do so in his instructions and examples—his commendation of Epaphroditus (2:25-30), his statements about his own life (3:7-11), his condemnation of the enemies of the cross of Christ (3:18-19), his appeal to Euodia and Syntyche (4:2-3), and his promises to the Philippians in relation to their sacrifices (4:15-19). In all these cases, honor and glory are based on a willingness to sacrifice and serve. But the supreme example is clearly Jesus, here highlighted as the King who has masterfully demonstrated the inviolable ways of his own Kingdom.

RE-ENVISION YOUR PATH

Many Christians have received this truth. Fewer have lived it. Maybe that's because the way of the world seems so much more reasonable. But perhaps it's also because of a misunderstanding. Humility does not mean letting yourself be abused, trampled on, or exploited. It simply means honoring those around you as extremely valuable, deeply loved human beings. The love God has showered on us is meant to be shared. Serving people as Jesus did is the most powerful way to do that. And it's ultimately rewarded with the glory of his Kingdom.

If we look closely, we'll see that most of Paul's teachings in this letter can be tied to some element in this trajectory. Like Jesus, we are to become an incarnation of divine love and truth, serve the world and each other with humility, become obedient to the sacrifices God puts before us, and live as those who will be (and already have been) seated with Christ in heaven (Ephesians 2:6). All of life—our thoughts, behaviors, desires, relationships, sense of calling, everything—takes on a different hue when this trajectory becomes our template. God not only approves of this life; he also empowers us to live it out and walks with us every step of the way.

THE COST OF GLORY

He did not think of equality with God as something to cling to.

2:6

We hate to see something valuable wasted—a promising career, a hidden masterpiece, lost years, an undeveloped talent, a missed opportunity. We lament what could have been because we know how rarely some promises, treasures, talents, and opportunities come around. We want people, including ourselves, to reach full potential, and we cringe when they (or we) don't.

But what if that career was "wasted" by someone who could have earned millions but chose instead to pour out their life on the mission field? Or that "hidden" masterpiece was really stowed away for preservation and restoration, only to be unveiled one day for more to see? Or those "lost" years were dedicated to grueling work that was eventually rewarded with a gold medal? Or that talent was undeveloped in order for that person to focus on another one with more significance? What if some opportunities were missed due to the pursuit of others with greater impact? Waste is in the eye of the beholder. And we behold a lot of things that seem like losses until we realize the gains they led to.

This idea essentially describes what Jesus did in coming to earth. Leaving behind the privileges of deity in order to live as a human seems ludicrous until we realize that his humanity made possible the restoration of our humanity.

Sacrificing himself on a cross makes no sense until we understand that he did so "because of the joy awaiting him" (Hebrews 12:2). Planting a seed in the ground for it to "die" seems pointless if it were not to flourish later in fruitfulness (John 12:24). Jesus' death was no mere example, a demonstration of sacrifice to prove a point. There was a payoff. Glory costs something. Infinite glory costs infinitely.

This is a dynamic of the Kingdom. If we set our focus only on the cost, we lose sight of the benefit. We spend our lives in drudgery, carrying a cross as though it never leads to a resurrection. But if we focus on the glory—if we see the benefit more than the cost—we live with energy and anticipation. We stop clinging to whatever we think we deserve and fix our eyes on the joy set before us. We're willing to make sacrifices for greater gain.

RE-ENVISION YOUR INVESTMENT

Even the world understands this principle. People live on a budget now in order to live off their investments later. Athletes impose discipline on their bodies in order to enhance their abilities. Students dedicate years of study in order to set themselves up for a worthwhile career. We know what it means to sacrifice for a gain.

But the Kingdom raises the stakes. Many find it hard to sacrifice what natural eyes can see in the here and now for what only spiritual eyes can see in eternity. Yet that's what Jesus did and calls us to do too. We can rest assured that the payoff is always worth it. In God's Kingdom, the benefits are always greater than the costs (Romans 8:18; 2 Corinthians 4:17). The pain of the journey never outweighs the beauty of the destination. Momentary sacrifices are investments with eternal interest. Setting our eyes on glory now ensures a life that, regardless of its troubles and twists and turns, will lead to that glory.

THE STORY'S END

At the name of Jesus every knee should bow, in heaven and on earth and under the earth, and every tongue declare that Jesus Christ is Lord, to the glory of God the Father.

2:10-11

Romans had a clear understanding of lordship. "Caesar is Lord" was a statement of loyalty required of any whose allegiance to the empire was questioned. Jews and Christians could not say such a thing without denying their own faith, which made their faith highly suspect in the eyes of authorities. Their "foreign" religion largely excluded them from the cultural mainstream. They were seen as people who simply didn't understand how the world works.

According to Paul, however, Christians understood exactly how the world works. Behind the scenes of rising and falling empires and their ego-driven leaders stands a far greater Lord. Roman and Hellenistic cultures were the ones outside the mainstream—not in the context of their own passing society but in the context of the entire universe. Rome's emperors may have thought they were living in the big picture, but relatively speaking, they were in a tiny, misguided world. Their vision was woefully inadequate for grasping ultimate reality.

Much of the letter to this point has been aimed at reorienting the vision of believers who may have lost their focus on that reality. It's easy in day-to-day experience to let small things loom large and large things fade away. But all existence is oriented around the fundamental truth of the triune God, with

Jesus exalted as the one Lord to whom every knee must bow. There is no picture larger than that—no greater agenda, no more pressing issue, no more ultimate purpose. All who have already embraced that reality by faith can rest assured that their life is headed in the right direction—regardless of what "mainstream" culture says.

Whatever adversity the Philippians were facing, whatever strife they were dealing with, whatever sacrifices they needed to make, in whatever ways they needed to endure, they could rely on the certainty that all human history, including their own lives, would culminate in universal acknowledgment of the only Lord who matters. Compared to that, everything else is mere details. The small story of their lives often distorted reality. The big story would keep them grounded.

RE-ENVISION YOUR STORY

This is true for us as well. We may get caught up in the details of life, and sometimes those details provoke uncertainty, insecurity, discouragement, or strife. The eternal vision fades into the background of our lives, and our spiritual myopia twists our desires, infects our relationships, and leaves us longing for more. The solution, of course, is to keep the eternal vision front and center. Seeing the big picture is a choice. Whatever story we think we're living in will shape our lives, so it's vital to get the story right. Ours is never one of defeat or meaninglessness. We have become part of an eternal display in heaven and on earth that Jesus is Lord, and one way or another, in time and eternity, that display will be visible for all to see.

PHILIPPIANS 2:12-18

LIVING THE KINGDOM

Paul's words in the previous six verses—or perhaps those of an early hymn he quoted—cast a vision of the ultimate sacrifice, the downward then upward trajectory of a life poured out for others and highly exalted forever. This next section serves as an important application of that example. The example of Jesus (and of Paul, as he describes himself in 2:17) has enormous implications, both for the believers' own fellowship and for their witness to the city of Philippi.

Paul reinforces these implications by reminding the Philippians of how obedient they have been to his instructions in the past and certainly will continue to be (2:12). Then he describes what it means to live out their salvation. Doing so is important not just for them but also for the world around them. They are positioned to be examples of the radical paradigm shift their culture so desperately needs. And when they realize that God himself is within them to shape, empower, and propel them (2:13; see also Ephesians 3:20)—that his irrepressible love and energy are advancing his Kingdom through them—they step onto the stage of their world as radiant displays of his nature.

BACKGROUND

Certain challenges come with that role. Philippians (and Romans in general) looked down on "eastern" religions, including Judaism and Christianity (see Acts 16:20-21). Paul himself was accused of being a troublemaker while in Philippi and left in order to keep the peace, so he understood how their ministry and witness could ruffle feathers. Their job was to defy stereotypes however possible—by living in harmony, being content, refusing to blend into pagan society, and generally making themselves uncriticizable insofar as they were able. They would stand out in the best way possible. They did not have the option of demonstrating God's Kingdom in a friendly environment. They were empowered to radiate Kingdom life into a dark and distorted world.

THE BIG PICTURE

For Paul, this need to demonstrate God's Kingdom meant that his work "was not useless" (2:16). He and they had worked hard to grow into the fellowship they had become. He didn't want them to lose the ground they had gained. Paul had spent himself for that cause and implied that they should too. The result, as with so much else in this letter, would be joy that he and they could share.

Kingdom communities exist not just for the building up of believers. They are also outposts of heaven in a hellish sort of world. When they function as designed, filled with God's presence and power, they draw many people in. When their members lose sight of that vision and operate as just another human organization, they don't. That makes reliance on God's presence and power the highest priority in the community of believers. Immersing ourselves in the flow of his Spirit demonstrates our salvation, expands our influence, and makes us shine in a dark world.

This passage points to the arena in which we live as carriers of God's Kingdom. This is where the divine trajectory (the "going down to go up") plays out. Anyone can demonstrate aspects of the Kingdom when all is going well, but God often puts his people in places of contradiction, where the grace, joy, peace, humility, and character of the Kingdom stand out by contrast. If we are going to make an impact by displaying the ways of heaven, it will have to be in the context of an unheavenly environment. Grace is only visible where it's needed; joy is only remarkable among the joyless; reconciliation only happens amid brokenness; and healing only comes to the wounded, not those who are well. The stage is set for God's people to reveal his nature through their own lives. And that makes every situation we face not a loss but a gain, an opportunity to be who we're called to be—and a cause for rejoicing.

Work hard to show the results of your salvation, obeying God with deep reverence and fear.

2:12

Imagine standing on one side of Niagara Falls, looking at a tightrope stretching across to the other side. Torrents of water roar as they rush over the precipice below. Your mission is to get to the other side by walking across the wire, and you've been assured by the God of the universe who holds all power in his hands that you will certainly make it across, without fail, by his guarantee. He will watch you every step of the way. But you have to go. Remaining on this side is not an option.

How do you feel as you inch your way across and see that terrifying tumult below? Even though you've been guaranteed safety, you make the journey with quite a bit of fear and trembling—not because you don't believe his promise but because you know how high the stakes are and how awesomely miraculous this endeavor is. When you finally get to the other side, you collapse in relief, heart still pounding, amazed at how you were protected along the way.*

God doesn't want you to feel quite that level of nervousness about living out your salvation, but he does want you to be aware of how wondrous and awe-inspiring it is. Some translations of 2:12 give the impression that our salvation

* This illustration was first used in the author's discussion guide written for Walk Thru the Bible: *A Walk Thru the Book of Philippians: Experience the Joy of the Lord* (Grand Rapids, MI: Baker, 2010), 32–33.

is still in question as we "work it out," but it's really a matter of living out what has already been accomplished, demonstrating the reality of Christ within us, the hope of glory (Colossians 1:27)—or, as the next verse tells us, recognizing that God himself is working in us to shape our desires and empower us.

God also wants this reverence to show up in our relationships. The phrase translated "reverence and fear" here is also used in 2 Corinthians 7:15 and Ephesians 6:5 in the context of human relationships, particularly with regard to honoring those in a higher position, which nicely complements Paul's instructions on humility in Philippians 2:3. Taking salvation or other people for granted does not fit the reality of what has happened to us. In short, the astonishing, jaw-dropping magnificence of redemption—being pulled out of the darkness and chaos of a fallen world and into the brilliance and beauty of heaven forever—should fill our hearts and minds and shape our spiritual relationships throughout our lives. Angels have longed to gaze at such things (1 Peter 1:12). Amazement fills the atmosphere of God's Kingdom.

RE-ENVISION SALVATION

That's a huge paradigm shift for those who tend to lose sight of what really happened when coming to Christ in faith. Some think of only the human implications, even if life-changing, and struggle to live out that decision daily in their own power. Some embrace the new identity in Christ that comes with that decision but grow weary struggling against any old identities that keep intruding. Few live with a constant awareness of the otherworldly implications of what happened on that cosmic stage—and the ongoing work of God in our lives (see 2:13). But holding that grand vision in our minds can be transforming. It causes much of our struggles and weariness to fade away in its glory. And it enables us to minister in a tumultuous world with the presence, power, and peace of God.

THE SPIRIT WITHIN

God is working in you, giving you the desire and the power to do what pleases him.

2:13

Try to envision the ultimate power center of the universe, the source from which a vast number of galaxies' worth of energy emanates. Surely this source pulses with unimaginable, explosive force exceeding that of billions of nuclear reactions, shines more brilliantly than human eyes could ever take in, radiates a heat more intense than human flesh could even begin to approach, and carries more potential than finite minds could ever conceive. We can hardly wrap our thoughts around such a prospect.

The ultimate power center of the universe is a Person, of course, not a thing. But he *is* that powerful and brilliant and intense, and even infinitely more. There's a reason Scripture shows us human flesh collapsing in his presence, falling before blinding light, and drawing back in shame in the face of such overwhelming purity. Apart from a supernatural work in our lives and the merciful covering of his glory for our sake, we could not come near him (see Exodus 33:18-23; 1 Kings 19:10-18). In our flesh, and especially when we were stuck in our fallen condition, we would melt away instantly.

Now imagine that ultimate power source being embedded within you. Mind-boggling, right? Incomprehensible. God at work within us is not just a Father tweaking the desires and impulses of his children—though he does that.

He is infinite wisdom, power, and love radically reshaping us from the inside out, if we will let him. The power that raised Jesus from the dead (Ephesians 1:19-20), the power that can do infinitely more than we can ask or imagine (Ephesians 3:20), is transforming us, directing us, and enabling us to do his works. This is the energy that drives us.

Don't shy away from that idea of being energized by God. Other belief systems may seem to have cornered the market on that word, but it's entirely biblical. The Greek term *energeō* is used here, in Paul's prayers in Ephesians (see above), and elsewhere to describe how God empowers us. He is planting his desires and purposes in his people, corporately and individually. Paul tells us here that this energizing is for his pleasure. We can take that in two ways: as us doing works that please him or as him being pleased in simply empowering us. In either case, the picture is not of people who are serving God by doing good things for him but of people who are serving with him to do good things. This is a partnership, and he is filling it with his divine energy.

RE-ENVISION YOUR SOURCE

Most people don't feel as if they are being energized by God himself. In fact, many distrust their desires and abilities and assume that they are by default contrary to God's will. We often have a remarkable tendency to trust our own ability to mess things up more than we trust his ability to keep us on track. Yet his Word declares that he is working within us to guide, preserve, and empower, shaping our will and giving us the means to carry it out. Our will blends with his, or his with ours, to live out his Kingdom in this world.

Let that energizing work of God's Spirit constantly come to the surface in your mind. Live with the awareness that the ultimate power of the universe is imparting his desires, purposes, and power into you through his Spirit. Trust that his will is becoming your will. Let yourself be driven by the work he is doing—for you, in you, and through you.

Do everything without complaining and arguing, so that no one can criticize you.

2:14-15

The picture Paul just painted for these believers was stunning. God himself, the creator and sustainer of the universe, was moving them, shaping their desires and wills, energizing their work in presumably (or at least potentially) supernatural ways. With this brilliant, intense power available within them, they had everything they needed to change the world.

Meanwhile, they were apparently complaining and arguing, perhaps getting hung up on personal conflicts, disputing doctrine, or struggling with living in an adversarial culture. They seem to have been anchoring themselves in the natural realm and all its clutter, expecting little supernatural intervention from God in their relationships with each other and their society. They were surrounded by perverse people (2:15) and apparently were being intimidated by their enemies (1:28), *yet the power of God was at work in them!* This dissonant picture of Spirit-empowered people not having the upper hand was completely unfounded. They had God himself within them.

This community in Philippi was not a troublesome fellowship, at least not nearly on the order of the Corinthians or some of Paul's other church plants. But it seems they needed a bigger vision. They needed to step out of their own little world of relatively microlevel turmoil and into the grand vista of what

God was doing not only in this world but in displaying the glories of his Son in seen and unseen realms. They may have thought they were just living in a pagan city and encountering some resistance. In reality, they were part of the divine drama playing out in front of heaven and earth and all their inhabitants, both human and divine, angelic and demonic, principalities and powers everywhere. They should not have been trifling with petty details. They were a vital part of God's much bigger agenda.

RE-ENVISION YOUR POSITION

The Philippians' situation and Paul's instructions for them are remarkably relevant to believers today. Many of us are living in a small, distorted picture, feeling confined by the limitations of our society and assuming those limitations are immovable. We are settling for marginal influence in our world, utilizing the natural weapons of the world and its rhetoric, finding those weapons and that rhetoric insufficient, and grumbling and disputing at many points along the way. We're living with eyes half closed.

Open them wide. Live out your salvation with awe. Dwell on the fact that God is at work within you to energize you and accomplish his plans for this world through you. Refuse the clutter and pettiness of little visions and weak self-perceptions. Know who you are as a citizen of heaven and live like it. You are, after all, a key player on the divine stage.

AS CHILDREN OF GOD

Live clean, innocent lives as children of God.

2:15

"Just a sinner saved by grace." That's the identity many Christians carry with them into every relationship and endeavor. They see themselves as fundamentally sinful but not as fundamentally changed. Grace has rescued them—barely—and they hope to grow in righteousness. But they can hardly imagine being "clean" and "innocent"—or, as some translations put it, "blameless." They may understand that Christ's righteousness has been imputed to them, but they don't really expect to live it out much. Those who see themselves as merely sinners saved by grace cannot become anything more.

Though that identity is theologically true, and the recognition of our sinfulness is foundational for how we enter into the Kingdom, it is not the whole story. God's plan for his people is redemption *and* restoration. We *were* sinners saved by grace. Now we're saints growing in the righteousness we've been given. We will undoubtedly sin, but that is a vestige of our past, not a defining characteristic. We are destined to become like Jesus, not only in the future when we see him face to face (1 John 3:2) but also increasingly in the present as we recognize that he is living and working within us (Philippians 2:13; see also Galatians 2:20; Colossians 1:27). The more we step into his fullness now, the more his fullness gets into us. But the complete spiritual DNA of Jesus is already there.

That's why Paul refers to believers as "saints" or "holy ones," those who are righteous and beloved—even when they have a long way to go in living out their righteousness. It's also why he was so confident that God would complete what he had started in these believers (Philippians 1:6). People's perceptions of their identity profoundly shape how they live. When we envision ourselves as sinners, essentially helpless to change, we become preoccupied with our sin. But a focus on sin never helps us get out of it. Only by gazing at something true and beautiful and good—and seeing ourselves in that image—can we grow into our new identity (2 Corinthians 3:18). Paul is not giving the Philippians instructions they cannot follow. He fully expects that they can live "clean, innocent lives."

RE-ENVISION YOUR IDENTITY

In this divine drama, do you see yourself as a character who is simply destined to remain flawed? "Just a sinner saved by grace" rather than someone who was a sinner but is now being restored and cleansed by grace? If so, may you embrace the identity Paul gives (Philippians 1:1). You are one of "God's holy people," no matter how unholy you might feel. You are already set apart. The spiritual DNA of Jesus is already implanted within you. You have the full potential of becoming more and more blameless, innocent, clean, and pure.

People live out whatever vision they have for themselves. If we see ourselves simply as sinners, we will continue to struggle mightily with sin. But if we see ourselves as God's own sons and daughters, and if that identity thoroughly and deeply sinks into our hearts, we will naturally grow more and more into his image. Incomplete theologies may assign us incomplete identities, but Scripture doesn't. We are completely, irrevocably, eternally children of God.

. . . shining like bright lights in a world full of crooked and perverse people.

2:15

God is, among other things, a blindingly brilliant light, and Jesus is the radiance of his glory. These images come alive from time to time in the pages of Scripture and have been confirmed by glimpses throughout history (see Ezekiel 1:26-28; Acts 9:3-9; 1 John 1:5). People who encounter him, who are given a view behind the veil of darkness that surrounds him (Psalm 18:11; 97:2), are dazzled.

It only makes sense, then, that God's people who are born of his Spirit would become bearers of light too. Just as there is no darkness in him (1 John 1:5), there is to be no darkness in us either. With God himself at work within us, we are endowed with the brilliance we need to shine in a dark world.

Paul's words here can be taken three ways, and each is true: (1) We are called to shine as good witnesses in order to win people to Christ. (2) We are called to shine in order to influence the culture around us with the nature of God's Kingdom. (3) We are called to shine as part of the cosmic display before heaven and earth of who Jesus is (Philippians 2:10-11). From Paul's words at various points in the letter, we can pick up on the likelihood that the Philippians were somewhat inwardly focused at the time, a little too preoccupied with their internal wrangling and cowed by whatever resistance their society was giving them. Their light was being dimmed by their own perspective.

Jesus inaugurated his Kingdom on earth but called his followers to continue doing the works he did and to advance his Kingdom to the ends of the earth. That's our mission, and it can be fulfilled only by God's power working within us. But there are two significant obstacles to that calling that have plagued Christians throughout history. These don't come from the resistance of the world, which is no match for God, but from within the hearts of his own people. One obstacle is that we have a limited view of ourselves as carriers of his Kingdom, host vessels for his Spirit. The other obstacle is related: We have often limited our vision to natural, human capabilities rather than raising our expectations for his intervention beyond the natural. We often pray big prayers but anticipate small answers, or even shrink the prayers to begin with. We don't see ourselves as we really are or fully grasp our role in his purposes.

RE-ENVISION GOD'S POWER

See with the eyes of the Spirit. You have an opportunity to pour life into the people around you. It won't happen if, like the Philippians, you become inwardly focused. But if you flip the switch from grasping for life to pouring life out, you not only experience more life yourself (Luke 17:33); you become a catalyst for changing lives and even changing your culture. You shine the light of heaven into a darkened generation.

Learn to see yourself as just that—a shining light, someone made in God's image who radiates brilliantly as he does, a culture-changer who stands out from the darkness and is not dimmed by it. The Philippians may have seen themselves as little lights trying to shine into a big, dark world, but even small lights make a big difference. Darkness can't overwhelm them; it always gives way to light. The Holy Spirit of the living God is working and shining within you, and you carry his Kingdom everywhere. At your core, as one reborn into his Spirit, you are fundamentally and forever supernatural.

POUR YOURSELF OUT

I will rejoice even if I lose my life, pouring it out like a liquid offering to God, just like your faithful service is an offering to God. And I want all of you to share that joy.

2:17

Jesus said, "If you cling to your life, you will lose it; but if you give up your life for me, you will find it" (Matthew 10:39). However that statement relates to salvation, it also expresses a very real here-and-now dynamic. While many people grasp for life wherever they can get it—the endless efforts to get more, do more, and be more testify to that—this never-ending reach actually saps the life out of us and causes us to miss the life God has put right in front of us in each moment. The real way to experience life, Jesus says, is to stop grasping and start pouring. The more you give of your life, the more you receive (Luke 6:38). If you can make the switch from taking in to flowing out, life in you and around you flourishes.

Paul had just suggested that the Philippians do something similar by shining light and life into their dark world. Now he once again points to himself as an example, albeit one who is following the vastly greater example he just described—Jesus pouring his life out in the Incarnation and reaping eternal fruit for vast multitudes of people. Paul has taken up the trajectory of Jesus, emptying himself and pledging to continue doing so. And even if that sacrifice ends in death, it is still a cause for joy. He was not interested in simply living as long as possible, prolonging his days and maximizing his lifespan. His goal was to maximize his fruitfulness. That's a totally different perspective.

Most of Israel's offerings were made with a portion left over for the priests to consume. Not so with drink offerings, the image Paul uses here. They were poured completely onto the altar, an apt symbol of what both Jesus and Paul had done. This is one way (among many others) Paul urges his readers to pattern their lives after him (see Philippians 3:17). He wants them to maximize their fruitfulness—and their life and joy—by holding nothing back. No matter what hindrances they may be sensing from within and beyond their fellowship, they are to give themselves extravagantly to the greater cause.

RE-ENVISION YOUR OFFERING

Nothing about that calling has changed. It's as true for us as it was for the Philippians. The attitudes, perspectives, and vision Paul demonstrated to the church at Philippi also apply to us today. The threatening power of everything they were facing—external opposition, internal discord, doctrinal threats, and more—would be thoroughly undermined by that overarching vision. Everything we face today is undermined by the same vision. The world holds no power over those who are willing to pour themselves out. In fact, power begins to flow from those who do.

PHILIPPIANS 2:19-30

SHINING EXAMPLES

Paul turns his attention to two men who were examples of what he has just described. Timothy and Epaphroditus had served with the humility of Jesus. They were not known for complaining and arguing. They were shining as lights in a world full of crooked people. Like Jesus and Paul himself, they were role models for the values and attitudes Paul has been teaching. So in addition to their position here as noteworthy subjects, they fit in the discussion of living out the values of the Kingdom as citizens of heaven.

BACKGROUND

These two exemplary figures also demonstrate Paul's vision for discipleship. He has utilized faithful workers throughout his ministry to teach believers, equip churches, and model the gospel. He has often sent Timothy to communicate with churches and check on how they are doing (1 Corinthians 4:17; 1 Thessalonians 3:1-8). Epaphroditus came from Philippi to deliver the church's gift and to minister to Paul, and even though he became ill and nearly died—not a convenient situation for an apostle in confinement—Paul considered him a co-worker. Throughout Paul's ministry, he showed a remarkable ability to entrust his work to people of various backgrounds, such as these two individuals—especially remarkable given the history of Jewish-Gentile relations—and they respected him as a bridge between the two cultures.

From the context here, it seems that Paul planned to send Epaphroditus back to Philippi very soon, carrying this letter with him. Then he would send Timothy sometime afterward to follow up and see how the church was doing—perhaps with regard to the instructions in this letter, but at least to offer further instruction and encouragement if needed. Then Timothy would return to Paul in Rome, filling him in with a firsthand account of their progress. Though the journey between the two cities was not short, this is how first-century communities remained in contact with each other.

THE BIG PICTURE

Citizens of God's Kingdom are called to embody its virtues and values. Timothy and Epaphroditus were doing that, and as images of Kingdom life, their example serves as an invitation for others to follow. (In Scripture, examples are always invitations.) If the Philippian believers accepted that invitation, they would shine as lights in their world, themselves becoming an invitation for others to enter into this Kingdom of light. A focus on self distracts from that message. A life of humility, service, and sacrifice magnifies it. Just as Paul foregrounds these men as examples, God wants to foreground the believers in this community to demonstrate what his Kingdom is like.

PLANNING WITH GOD

If the Lord Jesus is willing . . .

2:19

For the second time in this letter (see 1:21-25), we see Paul in the process of discerning God's will, and again, he gives no indication that his own will is completely taken out of the equation. He understood that he was to align with God's purposes, not the other way around, but he also understood that God invites the desires of his people into the conversation. Paul had his preferences and God had his, and frequently they overlapped. If they didn't, Paul would go with God's flow. But often they flowed together.

This verse indicates that Paul hoped or trusted in the Lord Jesus that Timothy would be able to go soon. He wasn't wondering whether sending Timothy might be God's will, although, as with everything, Paul held the details of the future loosely. He anticipated that this would happen—that Timothy would soon make a journey to Philippi to encourage these believers, see how they were doing, and then return with news for Paul. Later, he expresses even more confidence that he himself will be able to visit them—another expression of his certainty that he will be delivered from his present confinement (2:24). In each case, Paul assumes that his heart is in sync with God's. He trusts that his will and the Father's are aligned, even while recognizing that circumstances might work out differently.

This confident trust is what enables Paul to fill his letter with expressions of joy even while experiencing discouragement at his sense of being isolated, frustrated, and stressed: "I have no one else like Timothy" (2:20), "all the others care only for themselves" (2:21), "then I will not be so worried about you" (2:28). No matter what is going on in his immediate situation, he anticipates God's good purposes. But this is more than just a cognitive theological assurance that God was doing something good, whatever it happened to be. These purposes were written into Paul's heart. He knew and believed what to expect, at least in the big picture if not in the details, and those expectations were encouraging.

RE-ENVISION GOD'S PLANS

Recognizing that God is sovereign over everything and working all things together for the good of his people (see Romans 8:28) frees our spirit to acknowledge problems and hardships while simultaneously rejoicing over whatever God is doing in them. If we see our desires and God's plans as completely distinct and rarely overlapping, with him leaving us in the dark about whatever he is going to do, we grow discouraged. But if we realize he has placed his purposes in our hearts (Philippians 2:13)—that he much prefers to work through us rather than around us—we live with anticipation of his good and pleasing will. We can hope and trust that our hearts are in sync with his and can plan accordingly. When he gives us insight into his plans, we can cling to those plans in confidence. But even when we have to hold the details of the future loosely, we can know he holds us firmly and leads us in his will.

HEARTS IN SYNC

All the others care only for themselves and not for what matters to Jesus Christ.

2:21

Paul was clearly fond of Timothy and highly valued his partnership. In fact, Timothy was a coauthor of this letter (1:1), and though Paul couldn't put feet to his ministry while in Rome, Timothy could. He represented Paul in various ways, visiting churches and conveying Paul's words of wisdom. Paul trusted him.

One of the reasons Paul trusted Timothy was that Timothy shared his heart. Like Paul, he "genuinely care[d] about" the Philippians' well-being (2:20). Not only was he on the same page with Paul in understanding and methodology, as implied in their close ministry partnership; he was also on the same page at an emotional level in his concern for the people they ministered to. Like Paul, he seems to have had the affection of Jesus for this church (1:8). Following the example of both Jesus and Paul, Timothy himself was an example of what Paul had been writing about to this point in the letter, as he cared "for what matters to Jesus." Timothy was not looking out for his own interests (see 2:4). He had proved himself, acting like a son to Paul (2:22). And God was clearly at work in him, shaping his desires and energizing his work (2:13).

The same cannot be said of other co-workers of Paul, those who "care only for themselves." Paul had commended some co-workers and fellow believers who were (or had been) with him in Rome, both in this letter (1:14; 4:21-22) and in others (Ephesians 6:21; Colossians 4:7-14; Philemon 1:23-24), and surely he had not turned sour on these faithful companions. But he had also mentioned ambitious preachers whose motives were off (Philippians 1:15-17). Whoever he's referring to here, Timothy stood in stark contrast to them.

From this description, as well as many others in Paul's letters (including those to Timothy himself), Timothy lived with an orientation toward Christ. He sought Jesus' desires above his own, felt the compassion and affection of Jesus, and demonstrated the divine trajectory of humility that Jesus had modeled (see 2:5-8). He sought to live in sync with his Lord.

That's why Timothy was fruitful, useful to Paul, and an example of Jesus. And that's how we become fruitful, useful examples too. It's one thing to strive only to follow Jesus' instructions; it's another thing to synchronize with him. One approach easily becomes legalistic and leads to burnout; the other leads to transformation (which then results in living out Jesus' instructions). It's far better to merge with him in heart and mind, unite with him in the Spirit, be sensitive to the flow of his leading, be moved and empowered by him, and therefore shine his light effectively into the world. His truth then becomes much more than an instruction manual. It shapes us from within.

RE-ENVISION DESIRES

Much of our discipleship, perhaps even most of it, involves reorienting our desires. To follow Jesus, our hearts need to synchronize with his. Then, rather than constantly trying to beat down or reshape our desires, we can live out of the ones he has given us. When his affections, interests, and purposes freely flow within us, we freely flow in the directions they take us. We are driven forward by what concerns him. And because it is what concerns him, it is accompanied by his presence and power.

Saturate your heart and mind in the cares of Jesus. Like Timothy, fill your life with what matters to him. When you soak in his Spirit, what matters to him will become plain, and you will sense his presence in it. And your fellowship with him will become ever richer, more satisfying, and more abundantly fruitful.

WORDS THAT AFFIRM

Like a son with his father, [Timothy] has served with me in preaching the Good News. . . . [Epaphroditus] is a true brother, co-worker, and fellow soldier. And he was your messenger to help me in my need.

2:22, 25

Paul considered Timothy and Epaphroditus to be his co-workers. Timothy was one of his closest; he had traveled with Paul, served with him in ministry, proven himself trustworthy, and allowed Paul to mentor him over many years. Epaphroditus had brought the Philippians' gift to Paul in Rome and remained with him for some time, probably to help meet Paul's needs as he was able. They were all serving on the same mission to extend God's Kingdom wherever they could and to whomever would receive it.

Yet Paul saw both of these men as something more than co-workers, missionaries, or fellow soldiers. The Kingdom is not just an enterprise; it's a family. Timothy was like a son, and Epaphroditus was like a brother. These were not just men under Paul's (and God's) marching orders. They were family members who shared unbreakable bonds. Regardless of where they served and how often (or not) their paths crossed, they were related—sons of the same Father, filled with the same Spirit, sharers of the same spiritual DNA.

That familial relationship gives added weight to this section of the letter. The words Paul uses in his commendations of Timothy and Epaphroditus are filled with respect and honor. Whatever differences or tensions they may have had—most relationships have some of both, though we don't know any specifics in theirs—Paul affirmed and supported them. He built them up in the eyes of the Philippians. He recognized the treasure God had put in each of them.

RE-ENVISION AFFIRMATION

The world is full of people in need of someone to tell them they are important, valuable, and appreciated. Many assert their own importance, but this is often just posturing, a hope that their own voice will affirm what they need to know. Meanwhile, we know the truth that God values everyone. And when we express his heart, that value comes through.

We speak powerfully into people's lives when we affirm them. Sometimes affirmation isn't the first thing we think of—some people's flaws tend to stand out, and not everything they do should be affirmed. But there is always a treasure inside, some God-given talent, gift, desire, or hunger that is worth commending. Our affirmation can awaken them to God's voice—the call of significance he designed them for. Seeing people with God's eyes can draw them into his Kingdom.

But this is especially important within the Kingdom family. We are called to always build up fellow believers, never tear them down. Paul found it easy to affirm Timothy and Epaphroditus—there was a lot to admire in each—but even in our more difficult relationships, we have the opportunity to bless. Honor characterizes the Kingdom, and our words are to resound with it always.

A LIFE OF SERVICE

He certainly was ill; in fact, he almost died. But God had mercy on him—and also on me, so that I would not have one sorrow after another.

2:27

"Dying is even better," Paul wrote in Philippians 1:21, and Epaphroditus almost experienced that firsthand while in Rome. But like Paul, he would live on for further fruitfulness—God's act of mercy on him and on Paul, who recognized that as wonderful as it is for someone to depart and be with Christ, it's hard on those left behind.

Ancient travel conditions could be rough on the human body, and Epaphroditus may have taken ill even before he arrived in Rome. As welcome as his visit might have been, he may have become a burden to Paul, who was in no position to care for a diseased or dying man. Whether or not that was true, it was time for Epaphroditus to return. The Philippians would be delighted to see him again, and Paul would be relieved that he was reunited with them. He had served his purpose well in expressing the Philippians' concern for Paul and in carrying this letter back to them.

Paul did find Epaphroditus useful as one more example of the humility of Christ he spotlighted earlier in this chapter. Jesus had willingly sacrificed his life for others, and "God elevated him to the place of highest honor" (2:9). Epaphroditus almost died in his service to Paul on behalf of the Philippians, and now Paul wanted them to "give him the honor that people like him deserve" (2:29). If this church had any doubt that the divine trajectory of humility to exaltation was repeatable in the lives of people they knew, they no longer needed to wonder. It was playing out in the experiences of Paul, Timothy, and Epaphroditus, all of whom were making enormous sacrifices and were being honored in one way or another by other believers voicing God's affirmation. This was how believers were called to serve one another.

RE-ENVISION SACRIFICE

If you've ever viewed sacrifice as a loss, reconsider its role in God's Kingdom. It is the currency of devotion, given foremost to God but also to those who serve him. Our sacrifices demonstrate the nature of Jesus, build up his people, meet practical needs, bind us together in unity, and make a statement about the kind of Kingdom we are part of and how radically different it is from the ways of the world. As Paul so remarkably stated earlier, even the ultimate sacrifice of one's life is a gain, not a loss. Surely our lesser sacrifices are gains as well.

Living with a sacrificial spirit may seem unappealing, but it's actually a means to fulfillment. Epaphroditus returned to Philippi with honor and a sense of purpose. If his example spurred the Philippians to serve each other more humbly and better demonstrate God's nature to their city, then they certainly found a greater satisfaction in their fellowship and their calling. That's how God's Kingdom works, and humble service is how we experience its fullness. In God's economy, all our sacrifices serve a greater purpose, and all our losses become gains.

HONOR

Welcome him in the Lord's love and with great joy, and give him the honor that people like him deserve.

2:29

Honor is a characteristic of God's Kingdom. Any fellowship of believers that resembles the Kingdom should be filled with it—members of the community lifting each other up, affirming each other's gifts and service, valuing what each person brings to the table, and creating an environment of encouragement and support. That's essentially what Paul urged these believers to do at the beginning of this chapter (2:1-4). His instructions to work together with one mind and esteem each other highly describe a culture of honor. In a competitive and insecure world, people might tear each other down. But in the Kingdom, honor for everyone—not just those with great achievements—makes a fellowship strong.

Giving and receiving honor in Greek and Roman societies was a big deal, especially in patron-client relationships (where clients were expected to honor patrons) and in honoring achievements and public works. People of status eagerly sought such honor; in many cases, their generous sacrifices were not all that sacrificial, as they expected to be honored for them. Honor was the currency of power.

Paul spread honor much broader, and he honored people for things that would have been disregarded or even disparaged in the prevailing culture.

Sacrificial service, especially for low-status people (like a prisoner of Rome) or in the name of a marginalized religion (like Christianity), was not particularly admirable in ancient societies. But in the fellowship of God's Kingdom, it was. Or at least it should have been.

That's one reason Paul deliberately highlights the honor due to Epaphroditus for his costly service. What might have drawn sneers from a Roman guard or a Roman-Hellenistic culture like Philippi was actually highly esteemed in God's Kingdom. Having just told the Philippians to honor each other (2:1-4), Paul now gives them a couple of examples of what honor looks like. His words about Timothy and Epaphroditus demonstrate the kind of esteem that should mark God's people. He wants this church to envision a community filled with honor—and flourishing because of it.

So Paul uses the language of praise to lift up this brother who, in spite of his good work, seems to have become a heavy concern. He calls him a "true brother, co-worker, and fellow soldier" (2:25)—the last descriptor being particularly meaningful to a community like Philippi, with its military affiliations. These words put Epaphroditus on equal footing with Paul, affirming his heart, effort, and sacrifices as pleasing offerings to God. Paul provides an example of the kind of esteem he was calling for in the fellowship as a whole.

RE-ENVISION THE POWER OF WORDS

In any age, mutual expressions of honor create a culture that flourishes. While churches can thrive or fail for a variety of reasons, the issue of honoring each other—regardless of status or position—is often a key factor. We are drawn in directions where we are affirmed; everyone wants to be valued and esteemed. People feel at home in fellowships that honor and esteem well. They also hear in that affirmation the voice and heart of their Father building his people as one.

THE PRIORITY

He risked his life for the work of Christ, and he was at the point of death while doing for me what you couldn't do from far away.

2:30

When people make a long, productive, meaningful, satisfying life their primary goal—which could be said of the majority of human beings—they seek to arrange their lives to prioritize longevity and worthwhile experiences. Many Christians seem to include Jesus as simply a part of that planning. He becomes a means to the goal, a supplement mixed in with the vision of how our lives should play out. We all do that to a degree; human motives are always an obscure blend of the ideal and imperfect. But this does place limitations on the sacrifices we're willing to make.

When the work of Christ is *the* goal—not just the primary one but the all-encompassing one—those limitations are removed. When we focus on the "infinite value" of knowing Jesus, as Paul would soon explain (3:8), everything else is expendable. Sacrifices start to feel less sacrificial. One supreme agenda becomes worth any cost.

We were created for such singular vision. We were designed in God's image to relate to him and worship him as the center of our lives, seeing him even as life itself. He is our source, our breath, the one in whom we live and move and exist (Acts 17:28). Our lives only make sense and only feel right and ordered and true when they are oriented around the one who gave us life in the first place.

For all we know, Epaphroditus was just as mixed in his motives as the rest of us are. But Paul's words about him draw attention to his sacrifice "for the work of Christ." His actions demonstrated his ultimate priority, the center of his world. Life and death are small matters in light of God's overarching purposes for this world and the universal display of his Son. Everything must revolve around that cause. Epaphroditus's near-death experience reflected that driving purpose. Like Jesus, he embraced the downward trajectory (Philippians 2:5-8), and here Paul lifts him up.

Paul seems to have assumed an obligation on the part of the Philippians to help him out in his confinement. The expense of imprisonment usually fell on the prisoner, who was typically in no position to pay. Paul would downplay his need in 4:10-17, but he lived in a communal society (much more so than ours) and understood that the Philippians should try to fill in "what was lacking" (2:30 in some translations). Individualists like us may have a hard time grasping early Christians' understanding of the fellowship as a family, but Paul saw these believers as brothers and sisters (or even children) who would certainly sacrifice for a father or brother. Epaphroditus carried out that sacrifice because it was "the work of Christ" on behalf of his people.

RE-ENVISION YOUR PRIORITIES

Let Jesus—his person, his nature, his desires, his purposes—take center stage in your life. Fill your vision with who he is and what he is doing. Have conversations with him about it; this is not an exercise in hypotheticals. Envision your spirit opening to his voice, his movements, his heartbeat, and let yourself be moved in that direction. When he is preeminent in your being, you'll instinctively do as he desires. And it may not even feel like a sacrifice.

PHILIPPIANS 3:1-16

ALL THAT MATTERS

Having described Kingdom life and its values and perspectives, Paul turns to whatever might distort it. Apparently some doctrinal issues or false teachings have raised questions in the fellowship, and Paul has harsh words for those who distract from the truth of the gospel and the simplicity of devotion to Christ. He makes it clear that his views are not merely theological or theoretical; they are rooted in experience. Paul lived much of his life in pursuit of God through Jewish teachings and traditions, only to discover the Jewish Messiah who fulfilled them. Knowing Jesus relationally, intimately, and passionately—not through outward signs, even those once ordained by God—is the ultimate purpose of our lives.

BACKGROUND

Circumcision was given as a sign of God's everlasting covenant with his people (Genesis 17:7, 13). So it only makes sense that Jewish believers would expect Gentiles who are being grafted into the Jewish community through faith in its Messiah to take on that sign—along with observance of the law of Moses—for themselves. But for many Gentiles and the Jewish apostles and teachers who ministered to them, questions remained regarding how universal this sign was intended to be—especially when the Holy Spirit clearly showed up to dwell in Gentiles who believed in Jesus prior to being circumcised (Acts 10:44-46; 15:8-9). Was circumcision an everlasting sign of the covenant? Or was it a sign of the everlasting covenant that had now been fulfilled in Jesus? Since he fulfilled the law on our behalf (see Matthew 5:17; Romans 8:3-4), was this sign of the covenant with Abraham still necessary? The answer, according to Paul throughout his letters and to the Jerusalem council in Acts 15, was that faith in Christ and the presence of the Holy Spirit at work in those who believe were the only signs needed.

Yet many Jewish believers still taught otherwise, and even though Philippi did not have a strong Jewish population, growing Christian communities like the one in Philippi were often confused by such teaching. Some Gentile believers may have been tempted to become Jewish for another reason too: Judaism, a recognized religion in the Roman world, was legally exempt from the emperor cult. Jews had therefore already been cleared from claiming Caesar as Lord. Early Christians were operating in a gray area between being a Jewish sect and a separate religion (this status was what was at stake in Corinth in Acts 18:5-17). But Paul wanted nothing added to the simplicity of believing Jesus. That alone—even above his own Jewish heritage—must be a Christian's only true passion.

THE BIG PICTURE

In contrasting the concept of "Jesus plus the Jewish law" with faith in Jesus alone, Paul cast a vision for his magnificent obsession, the single-minded, wholehearted, infinitely valuable pursuit of knowing Jesus. By comparison, all other pursuits are worthless rubbish or dung, distractions from the greatest prize of knowing him. Orienting oneself entirely around this pursuit leads to experiences of God's presence and power. Orienting around religious requirements, even those once revealed by God to his people, does not. Any distraction from the one worthy pursuit is problematic, even "evil" (Philippians 3:2), no matter how well intentioned. We are saved by, live by, rest in, depend on, are transformed by, and persist in the grace of God through faith alone. Our entire identity is forever wrapped up in Jesus, and we become one with him (3:9).

For that reason, Paul saw no reason to cling to the past (3:13). He maintained a forward-moving vision. Even though he already knew Christ and had deep, intimate fellowship with him, he realized there was more—a "heavenly prize" and a glorious "end of the race" (3:14), the outcome of the divine trajectory of humble descent followed by exaltation with Christ (Matthew 23:12; 1 Peter 5:5-6). For Paul, "what lies ahead" (3:13) lay behind everything he did.

FOR YOUR OWN GOOD

Whatever happens, my dear brothers and sisters, rejoice in the Lord. I never get tired of telling you these things, and I do it to safeguard your faith.

3:1

These sentences seem odd, not for what they say but for where they're placed. They're made even more conspicuously odd by the chapter and verse notations, which of course were not in Paul's original letter (neither were punctuation marks or clear sentence breaks at many points in ancient Greek texts). Paul's instruction to rejoice in the Lord is plain enough—he has said it before and will say it again (2:17-18, 28-29; 4:4)—but why here?

Is this a conclusion to everything Paul has written so far? Is it the third of three imperatives that began a couple of verses earlier ("Welcome him . . . give him the honor that people like him deserve" (2:29) . . . now "rejoice")? Is it an introduction to the next section, which will abruptly shift to something that seems hardly worthy of rejoicing? Or is it a stand-alone comment, inserted here because it happened to come to Paul's mind or perhaps because it began the original conclusion to this letter before he decided to keep going? We obviously can't ask him. Readers and commentators can only speculate about such things.

This command does clearly fit the previous discussion, not only in the last few verses but also almost from the beginning of the letter. Yet the fact that Paul sees it as beneficial for the Philippians—to keep them "safe" or help them remain steadfast—seems also to point to what is coming: a warning about teaching that could shake them off course and keep them from remaining steadfast.

In any case, whether it is looking back at previous text or ahead to what follows (or both), it is yet another example of the importance of rejoicing in the midst of ostensibly negative circumstances. Paul has already made it abundantly clear that negative circumstances aren't all that negative when you see the big picture—imprisonment, rival preachers, the possibility of execution, intimidating opposition, hardships, and sacrificial service all fit one way or another into God's miraculously redemptive and restorative work. The things that look threatening are not threatening at all to those who are anchored in eternity and living in light of the final revelation of Jesus. For people with eyes of faith, there is something of joy to see in almost everything.

RE-ENVISION REJOICING

We are called to a joy-saturated life. This is not the last time in this letter Paul emphasizes joy, and clearly he believes it is central to the Christian life and to the Philippian fellowship. All that they were going through could be remedied or at least eased by this attitude. They would not have to wait for joy to come to them; otherwise Paul wouldn't command it. They had a choice in the matter, and we do too.

That choice largely involves looking at and thinking about the right things. Our focus stirs our hearts, for better or worse. And if we really understand who God is, who we are, what he has promised us, what our glorious future entails, and that he has worked in our lives and continues to do so, joy comes naturally. Such a focus transforms us, and it transforms the people around us. In more ways than one, it brings the Kingdom to earth.

A VISION OF THE GOSPEL

Watch out for those dogs, those people who do evil, those mutilators who say you must be circumcised to be saved.

3:2

Across numerous ancient cultures, *dogs* was an insult. Greeks and Romans used the term to disparage foreigners. Jews used it to disparage Gentiles (and even unworthy Israelites, as in Psalm 22:16 and Isaiah 56:10-11). So when Paul directs the term at false teachers and makes it clear that they were advocating for circumcision, he is turning a common insult against people who had probably used the insult many times themselves.

Were the Philippians being threatened by Jewish believers who were trying to convince them, like the Galatian believers, that they needed to become fully Jewish in order to be fully Christian? The fact that Paul could find no synagogue there on his first visit—apparently the city did not have the requisite ten Jewish men to form one—tells us there was little Jewish influence there (Acts 16:13). But perhaps Jewish Christians had passed through, as they had elsewhere, and were trying to add this doctrine to the gospel of grace. Either way, Paul felt that the presence of false teaching along these lines was strong enough to warrant a warning to this community.

The key question was whether someone could be included in the covenant of Abraham without taking on the sign of that covenant. Non-Christian Jews and many Jewish Christians would have said no. Paul and the council at

Jerusalem (Acts 15) said yes. Yet the debate still raged and often centered around the matter of circumcision—according to Scripture, the sign of an *everlasting* covenant (Genesis 17:7, 13), which implies it could not be done away with. Even Jesus said that not one detail of the law would pass away (Matthew 5:18). Paul and other like-minded believers argued that the law hadn't passed away; rather, it had been fulfilled in Christ and served its purpose. And, as Paul argues in Galatians, the law came after the covenant with Abraham, which was meant for all nations, and did not cancel out that earlier covenant (Galatians 3:8–5:6). But some could not see or would not agree with such arguments.

Yet the entire vision of the gospel was at stake. A person can see salvation as conditioned on obedience or as a gift received by faith, not some of both. Obedience is an appropriate response to salvation—most would have agreed to that—but it isn't a prerequisite for it. This was not a minor theological difference. Paul's harsh language tells us that the stakes are extremely high. He wanted all who read his words to put every ounce of their confidence in what Jesus did for them, not in what they could do for themselves.

RE-ENVISION YOUR FREEDOM

That notion goes against human instincts. We've been well trained in the idea of results-oriented performance. We can cling to that idea if we want to, but only if we understand that it's Jesus' performance that achieved the results. Everything in the Christian life originates with him, is worked into our lives through his Spirit as we believe (Philippians 2:13), and plays out as we live our salvation with faith-filled awe and reverence (2:12). We don't have to perform, which is wonderful news, since our performance always falls short. We're not under pressure to prove ourselves, since God has already identified us as his children, born of his Spirit through faith in Jesus. We are forever free—thoroughly saved, fully accepted, and completely empowered by him. And for that, our rejoicing never needs to end.

We who worship by the Spirit of God are the ones who are truly circumcised. We rely on what Christ Jesus has done for us. We put no confidence in human effort.

3:3

If we were to observe someone regularly performing extensive religious rituals, we might consider them very faithful. They would appear devoted, and we could probably assume that they were. We would know little about the condition of their heart, other than the presumption that at whatever point they embraced their faith, it was probably sincere. But was their heart still in it now? Had substance turned into mere form? We wouldn't know. Their performance would only serve as a sign that at some point—and perhaps still in the present—they were committed to their beliefs.

If we were to observe someone passionately worshiping God, manifesting the presence of his Spirit in their worship and daily lives, we'd have little doubt about their commitments. Some people can fake such devotion, but usually not by daily, continually pouring out their hearts in love for the one they worship. We would likely consider such heartfelt and persistent displays of devotion as genuine, vibrant, and compelling. Their worship would serve as a sign of their relationship with him.

The point of circumcision was to mark God's people as set apart to him. It was an act of dedication to the covenant he established with them. But while it's possible to be circumcised without being dedicated to God or his covenant, it isn't possible to be filled with *Spirit-inspired* worship without being dedicated to him and his covenant. If the Philippians were looking for a sign of devotion, that was the clearest one.

God's covenant with his people is always foremost about relationship, not ritual. He wasn't opposed to rituals—he prescribed quite a few—but they were never the substance of the relationship, only its markers. When God's Spirit inhabits his people, worship itself becomes the sign of faith and a manifestation of his presence and power in our lives.

RE-ENVISION WORSHIP

This reality implies, of course, that our worship is strong and clear enough to be a sign. Apparently in the community of believers at Philippi, it was. Encounters with God through his Spirit are not always tangible, but many times they are, as evidenced throughout the book of Acts. The argument of Paul and other apostles that Gentiles were fully saved and in relationship with God apart from circumcision and the law was based on rather discernible manifestations of the Holy Spirit in Gentile believers' lives (Acts 10:44-46; 11:15-18; 15:8-9; 19:5-6). It was the clearest evidence that God's Spirit was present and hearts had been changed. It was the overflow of what faith in Jesus accomplished in the human spirit.

Worship is an experience with God and an offering of praise and devotion to him, but it's also a testimony. It reflects the throne room of heaven—always a fitting atmosphere for Kingdom citizens. Sometimes it will be deeply private, sometimes corporate; often internal, but also visible and demonstrable at times. After all, worship in heaven is magnificently tangible (see Revelation 4–5). On earth, it can serve as a sign of our connection with that glorious environment. It brings that environment into the situations and circumstances of our lives, transforming us (and often our circumstances) in the process—an experience Paul could emphatically confirm based on his first visit to Philippi, when God responded to his praise with a liberating earthquake. And it's a vital, persuasive demonstration of hearts in love with their God.

A NEW CONFIDENCE

I could have confidence in my own effort if anyone could. Indeed, if others have reason for confidence in their own efforts, I have even more!

3:4

After years of striving for holiness and fruitfulness, disciplining himself to become all God had called him to be and do in China, missionary Hudson Taylor had a sudden realization. If Jesus was truly living in him, as he believed, and had in essence exchanged lives with him (see Galatians 2:20), all he had to do was rest and let Christ live through him. The way to fruitfulness was not harder, deeper, more intense work; it was trusting in the power of Christ to work through him. This was a thoroughly liberating realization that changed Taylor's life. Power flowed through him in a new way from then on.

Paul had learned the same truth, albeit in a different context. He learned the hard way that we can't do the works of the Spirit in the strength of the flesh. Obedience to the law—or any set of rules and instructions—doesn't change our state of being. Fallen human beings have no ability to generate pure, eternal fruit. Or, to put it another way, the dead can't raise themselves.

Just as Paul used his own example positively, he was not afraid to use it negatively. His reasoning in the next two verses is convincing: *You want to see what human works lead to? I did them with zeal, and the result was that I killed people who were filled with God's Spirit.* His well-intentioned flesh was not only insufficient; it also led in the wrong direction.

Grasping this reality comes down to two issues: how we see our own abilities and how we see God's. Given the disparity, why would anyone ever put their faith in their own accomplishments instead of what Christ has already accomplished? The only reasons are ignorance and pride. A person either underestimates human depravity or overestimates human capacity (or both). In any case, that vision needs to come crashing down—and often does when God allows someone to hit bottom so they might finally turn to him.

RE-ENVISION YOUR POTENTIAL

Once that happens, a new vision takes its place. Instead of trying to become a better version of ourselves, we become captivated with the possibility of being made entirely new. We no longer try to maximize our condition, marginally growing in our same old state. We leave one realm and step into another. We become new creations. We enter into a new genesis, the dawn of a new existence.

That's an entirely different picture of human potential, and it can only be accomplished by trusting in a power beyond ourselves to flow through us. God has declared us righteous based on Jesus' works and has implanted his Spirit within us. We experience that by believing it. Instead of being exhausted, we become reenergized. We realize that apart from our faith and our relaxed efforts to walk it out, all the energy and fruitfulness depends on him. Like Paul, we're set free from the futility of our own efforts and at rest in the power and goodness of God.

I was circumcised when I was eight days old. I am a pure-blooded citizen of Israel and a member of the tribe of Benjamin—a real Hebrew if there ever was one! I was a member of the Pharisees, who demand the strictest obedience to the Jewish law. I was so zealous that I harshly persecuted the church. And as for righteousness, I obeyed the law without fault.

3:5-6

Paul was clear in how he saw his world before encountering Christ. He was a Hellenistic Jew—born in the Jewish diaspora in Tarsus—thoroughly committed to the biblical story of God's everlasting covenant with his chosen people. Many of Jerusalem's Jews might not have seen him as a real Hebrew, considering his upbringing in a Greek city, but he certainly saw himself that way. Trained as a Pharisee, he zealously guarded Jewish faith, tradition, and culture, especially against the creeping influences of Hellenism and Rome. For Paul, this was clearly God's will as revealed in Scripture.

The problem was that Paul's clear vision of life and purpose was wrong. Like many Pharisees, he guarded the details of biblical revelation—along with Pharisaic traditions—but missed the big picture. Such a vision, so deeply entrenched in a person's heart and mind, doesn't change unless something dramatic happens. But something dramatic did clearly happen to Paul. He went from protecting God's people from outside influences to embracing a new mission as an outside influencer reaching far into foreign cultures.

The dramatic thing that happened was, of course, coming face to face with Christ in a "vision from heaven" (Acts 26:19). He met the risen, radiant Jesus while on a journey to persecute people who believed in Jesus, a meeting that redirected the course of Paul's life. Jesus commissioned this new apostle to take the message of God's Kingdom to Gentiles, the very people he had once sought to keep at arm's length as corrupting influences. Now this "real Hebrew" was arguing with other Hebrews about the Messiah, the covenant, and God's ultimate purposes for this world. And he was doing it in a way that embraced Greeks and Romans who hardly knew a thing about the Jewish experience.

An accurate view of who God is and what he is doing changes everything. It can turn enemies into advocates and persecutors into partners, and it can redirect the passion of zealots toward the right things. It rejoices in truth, proclaims freedom for captives, looks beyond natural limitations, and insists that miracles happen. And it fills people with an all-consuming desire to know and experience Jesus and all he wants to accomplish through his people.

That's where Paul is headed in this discussion because he wants the Philippians to have a taste of this dramatic reorientation he experienced. He knows that some already have; their lives had changed as they believed in Jesus, and they had become bright lights shining in a dark world. They had come out of pagan culture and into the Kingdom of God. But he wants them to sense the depth of this transformation and be captivated by his all-consuming passion. He understands that human beings live by vision far more than they live by instructions.

RE-ENVISION JESUS

Whatever you do, immerse yourself in a captivating vision of Jesus. Let your heart be filled with the infinite value of knowing him beyond all else. See his Kingdom and his presence as the treasures that make all costs worthwhile (Matthew 13:44-46), and reorient yourself around it completely. Pursue an ever-deepening love for him as the highest goal you could ever reach. There is no greater purpose in life.

A PRICELESS TREASURE

Everything else is worthless when compared with the infinite value of knowing Christ Jesus my Lord.

3:8

News spread rapidly when gold was discovered in California in early 1848, provoking a frenzied rush to get as much of it as possible. At first, people only came from nearby, but soon others were streaming in from seemingly everywhere—the eastern United States, Mexico, Hawaii, Peru, Australia, China, and more. Recognizing that a treasure was there for the taking, at least until the supply was exhausted, they left behind everything they knew—homes, jobs, farms, and families. They envisioned greater benefits from a few weeks or months of gold-seeking than they might gain from years of labor back home.

The treasure of knowing Christ is infinitely more valuable than gold, but that same kind of single-minded pursuit is what Paul has in mind here. He had left behind everything that was once valuable to him in order to gain knowledge of Jesus—not just information *about* Jesus, but an intimate fellowship *with* him. Compared to the surpassing value of that, everything else was practically worthless. Paul never gave up his Jewish identity. He preached in synagogues, observed the Sabbath, took vows, worshiped at the Temple, and supported certain rituals as normal expressions of faith. But he saw that entire identity and all that came with it as subordinate to knowing Jesus. He would not try to fit Jesus into the things he once valued; he would fit those things—or not, if they simply wouldn't fit—into his new identity in Christ.

There is nothing theoretical or purely theological about Paul's words here. He clearly is describing not merely a cognitive belief but a tangible, heartfelt, interactive relationship with Jesus. He would never have encouraged the Philippians or any other group of believers to simply believe the right things (although believing the right things is important). He wants them to be captivated by a vision of who Jesus is and a passion for following him daily. He seems to imply that if their experience of Jesus were more real and all-encompassing, many of their issues would fade away. They would be stronger in the face of adversity, less focused on personal inconveniences and conflicts, and more impactful in their city.

RE-ENVISION YOUR VALUES

Reexamining our priorities and our pursuit of knowing Jesus is a vital part of our life in him. What do we really value? Does that value show up in the way we spend our time, energy, and resources? More importantly, does that value show up in our hearts and minds? Does Jesus become distant in the midst of daily to-do lists? Or is he at the forefront when we wake up in the morning, lie down at night, and go about the day in between?

The answers to those questions tell us a lot about what we treasure in our hearts—and whether we are growing in Christ, walking in the power of his Spirit, and influencing our world with the ways of his Kingdom. If we truly see who he is, we orient our entire lives around him. We become captivated by the treasure that is there for the taking.

OUR HIGHEST CALLING

For his sake I have discarded everything else, counting it all as garbage, so that I could gain Christ and become one with him.

3:8-9

Jesus said that the greatest commandment is to love God with all our heart, soul, and mind (Matthew 22:34-38). If that's the greatest commandment, it's also our life's greatest purpose. And if it's our greatest purpose, then any time we look back on our day, our week, or our year and realize we were more preoccupied with other things, we have defaulted on our purpose. Everything else is secondary, but we have elevated the secondary over the primary. If we haven't foregrounded love for him in all we do, we've missed the point.

Paul arranged his priorities according to this purpose, not as a calculated discipline but as a passionate pursuit. He was investing himself in the things of God as an overflow of his devotion to Christ, not as a calculated ministry agenda. When he writes of knowing Christ, he is not just referring to knowing *about* him. He is well aware that Jesus is alive—that was settled on the Damascus road. But this "knowing" also involves interacting with and trusting the living Christ daily. Jesus was a strong presence in his life.

Paul didn't just count his Jewishness and all its trappings as loss. He counted *all* things as loss compared to knowing Jesus. Paul sacrificed everything he once had, even considering it garbage—a shocking statement for any Jewish person, even a Jewish Christian—for the sake of following Jesus. If Christ were put on one side of a scale and everything else in life on the other, Christ would always weigh more. He made everything else of value look a lot less valuable. Or, as an old hymn puts it, "The things of earth will grow strangely dim, in the light of his glory and grace."*

As much as Paul presents a theology in these verses, his focus is relational. He is demonstrating a truth he described in his second letter to the Corinthians: Gazing at the image of Jesus with unveiled faces has the effect of transforming us into that image (2 Corinthians 3:18). As important as self-discipline may be, Paul is talking about something more. A captivated heart changes a life from within.

RE-ENVISION YOUR SIGHT

That's a gaze worth pursuing. It may take some practice—most of us don't have an experience like Paul's of encountering the resurrected Jesus in his glory—but this holy preoccupation should be a cornerstone of our lives. It's the primary way to cultivate love for Jesus; and as we know, love for him is why we were made. We don't fulfill our purpose simply through a discipleship course, a ministry pursuit, or a network of fruitful relationships, as helpful and good as these are. We begin and end with the gaze toward Christ that stirs our love and draws us into the relationship we were created for. We not only become like him; we become *one with him*. From there God can do whatever he wants for us, in us, and through us. We are in him, he is in us, and we move together as the eyes of our hearts are fully focused on him.

* Helen H. Lemmel, "Turn Your Eyes upon Jesus," 1922.

ONE PATH TO CHOOSE

I no longer count on my own righteousness through obeying the law; rather, I become righteous through faith in Christ.

3:9

"Two roads diverged in a yellow wood," wrote the poet Robert Frost, and like travelers everywhere, he had to choose one or the other.* Our lives are like that. We can't go in every direction that might look appealing; in selecting one path, we're rejecting others. We can only make our choices as wisely as possible—with the inspiration of God's Spirit and godly counsel, we hope—and then try to live without regret. If we discover we made a bad choice, God gives us grace and steers us back, if we will let him. If we discover our choice was indeed the wise one, we count our blessings and give thanks.

Paul had made some catastrophically wrong choices, but he was eternally grateful for how Jesus led him into the right one. As his vision grew, he came to frame his primary choice as between two ways to seek righteousness, one of them futile, the other fruitful. He had long tried one and even considered himself "without fault" in it (3:6), so he wasn't driven away from it by any sense of guilt. But after meeting Jesus, he was aware that law-keeping wasn't enough. Though the law was from God, keeping it was still a matter of human effort. The other way to righteousness was to accept the work of

* Robert Frost, "The Road Not Taken," 1916.

someone who *was* truly righteous as his own—an offer Jesus makes to all who will receive him. And Paul was forever thankful Jesus opened his eyes to it.

Paul's point here and elsewhere is that if our calling is to become like Jesus and we're empowered by his Spirit to do so, why on earth would we need a law—a faint shadow of the real thing—to fulfill that calling? And if we're relying on a law—even the words of Jesus can become a "law" if we're simply trying to follow instructions without being changed—we aren't relying on the empowerment of his Spirit within us. The two modes of seeking righteousness work against each other. We can't choose both paths. And Paul was highly critical of those trying to do so—or choosing the inferior, futile path.

RE-ENVISION IDENTIFICATION WITH JESUS

Real righteousness, not just as a legal status but also as something we experience, comes from being "one with him" (literally, "found in him")—fully entering into Jesus' sacrifice and resurrection and fully identifying with him over all other loyalties. When we see ourselves in the person of Jesus as he went to the cross, died, and was buried—with all our sin going into the tomb with him—and then being resurrected with him, with death and sin left behind, we grow into that vision. What is true of us doctrinally becomes true of us in experience, a bit more each day. It's remarkably transforming. It may be a road less taken, but it's a choice no one can end up regretting.

PARTICIPANTS IN HIM

I want to know Christ and experience the mighty power that raised him from the dead. I want to suffer with him, sharing in his death.

3:10

Saul and his army were paralyzed by the taunts and threats of Goliath, the hulking Philistine warrior. They listened to his challenges daily, but no one had the nerve to take him on. Without even fighting, they were already defeated. When a young shepherd named David arrived at the front and expressed outrage at this insignificant giant's defiance of the living God, the king agreed to let him take that attitude—and a slingshot—into the valley to face the threat. As we know, David killed Goliath, and the Philistines were scattered (1 Samuel 17). Israel's entire army had done nothing to accomplish the victory, but every man received the victory's benefits.

That image of a vicarious victory is in some ways a picture of what Jesus has done for us. He won the victory; we get the spoils. We don't even have to fight that battle. There may be some cleanup operations, but the outcome is already decided.

Even so, Paul wanted to increase his participation in Jesus' victory, and Jesus had called for it when he told his followers they would take up their cross and be treated like their Master (Matthew 16:24). The victory is already won, and we already receive its benefits—Jesus took care of that, and we receive the benefits by faith—but that's not the same as *getting to know him*. We don't (or shouldn't) just want a distant, detached victory. We want to see it, taste it, and enjoy the spoils with him.

People grow deeper in relationships through shared experiences. We know Jesus more intimately when we share something of his death and resurrection and the sacrifice and power that was involved. Or, as Paul has already illustrated, when we embrace the attitude of Jesus in his downward then upward trajectory and apply it to our lives and relationships. We aren't just observers of the cosmic triumph accomplished by Jesus' incarnation, death, resurrection, and exaltation. We walk with him through it. The dynamics of opposition he faced are still at work in our world. Crosses, tombs, resurrections, and glory become part of a believer's experience.

RE-ENVISION FAITH AS EXPERIENCE

We are therefore called to have not just head knowledge of Jesus but also heart knowledge. He wants us to interact with him rather than just know about him. He invites our affections. He draws us toward him to be in deep relationship, to be increasingly in sync with his loves, joys, sufferings, desires, purposes, and all the depths and heights of his experience. We emulate him by humbling ourselves as he humbled himself in the Incarnation. We are no longer just human beings stuck in earthly turmoil. We are overcomers with him in the full range of spiritual, emotional, psychological, physical, and relational victories.

It's good to be a believer in Jesus. It's even better to be a participant with him. He never envisioned his people merely agreeing with the truth—though that's certainly part of it. He calls us to step into the truth—for him, with him, and through him. Yes, there may be a taste of death in that at times. But the tastes of resurrection and exaltation are far more exhilarating, lasting, and worthwhile.

. . . so that one way or another I will experience the resurrection from the dead!

3:11

Every race begins with a view of the finish line. Every sports season begins with the goal of a championship. Every construction project is shaped by the concept drawings. Every marketing campaign is driven by sales numbers. And every ministry is designed to reach certain outcomes. We know what it's like to be driven by an idea of the finish because that's how human beings are wired. We envision destinations. For a believer, that destination is the resurrection.

As some translations show, the language Paul uses in this sentence seems to suggest uncertainty—"if somehow I may attain to the resurrection from the dead" (NASB)—giving the idea that he might not attain to resurrection, though he hoped he would. Of course, this hardly fits with many of Paul's other statements in this letter and others. He already assured the Philippians that God would complete what he started in them (1:6) and would certainly believe the same for himself. So this verse must express not an "if" in the sense that the matter is still up in the air but rather a "since"—whatever sacrifice it took, he would participate in the resurrection. The apostle who wrote so eloquently about the resurrection in 1 Corinthians 15 maintained a certain hope that God would bring it about—but also a strong belief that *only* God could bring it about.

In any case, Paul was driven by this vision of resurrection. He wasn't just gazing at the infinite value of Jesus; he was gazing at the infinite value of the *resurrected* Jesus. This is where it's all headed for him and for everyone who believes. Just as certainly as Jesus was resurrected and exalted (Philippians 2:6-11), this is our ultimate hope.

With this end goal, Paul's whole life makes sense. Without it, it doesn't (1 Corinthians 15:13-19). This notion came through clearly in his discussion of how both living and dying were wins for him. He knew the end of his story. But he also knew he was still in the middle of it. Like him, we are called to live out our story with a view to its end.

When we don't know where we're headed, we live with a sense of randomness or half-heartedness. When we do understand where we're headed, we live with that purpose and its related priorities in mind. If you want to live a purposeful life, determine your values and set goals that fit them. But in your planning, be sure to focus on the resurrection and all it entails.

RE-ENVISION RESURRECTED LIFE

When you live with a clear view of the resurrection,

- "you only live once" loses relevance, and you don't feel compelled to spend all your time, energy, and resources grasping at life while you can get it;
- you are far more willing to make sacrifices and endure hardships because you know they are a mere blip on the screen of eternity;
- you begin to see people as redeemed, divinely inhabited, everlasting beings and treat them as sacred; and
- you're far more willing to invest yourself in eternity and seek fruit that lasts.

That's life-changing. The rest of the world is desperate for meaning. We have it. We know where we're headed and have every reason to be gleaming with hope every day of our lives.

A COMPLETE BUT COMING SALVATION

I don't mean to say that I have already achieved these things or that I have already reached perfection. But I press on to possess that perfection for which Christ Jesus first possessed me.

3:12

Envision being given an incredibly expensive, high-tech, high-performance car, fully loaded with features you've never seen, much less known how to use. It's got everything you could possibly want. It may take you a long time to learn how to make the most of it, and of course you'll still need to put gas in it and maintain it to keep it running as it should. But there's really nothing to add to it; it's a complete package. You can even begin driving it right away.

A lot of things come to us in complete packages but still require time and experience to fully appreciate, even in the natural world. Seeds have everything they need in them to become giant trees, though their development takes decades. Babies are full-fledged human beings, though they take years to grow and mature. There is nothing lacking in these marvels of creation; they are complete from day one. Yet their growth and development unfold over time, and they must be nurtured and cultivated to become fully formed.

Salvation is already a complete, fully sufficient package. There's nothing to add to it that isn't already included. Unpacking that package, however, is a lifelong process. Learning to walk in resurrection power and growing into the image of Jesus are pursuits, not transactions. Salvation comes to us in an instant, but the implications are manifold and ongoing. It is not just redemption but also restoration; not just a destination but also a journey; not just being born into the Kingdom but also learning what the Kingdom is all about and walking in Kingdom wisdom, power, and love in the context of Kingdom communities and a darkened world. The fullness of salvation unfolds over a lifetime because it applies to every area of our lives.

Paul's vision of progress began with receiving salvation in all its completeness but then stepping into it in increasing measure. As he pursued the infinite value of knowing Christ—as he fixed his eyes on Jesus (see 2 Corinthians 3:16-18)—he was being transformed. He knew it was an ongoing process. He hadn't yet arrived at the exact image of Christ, even though that image was already implanted in him.

RE-ENVISION WHAT YOU'VE BEEN GIVEN

That's our model. As we fix our eyes on Jesus to behold his glory and conform to it, we will naturally be spending less time fixing our eyes on whatever seems to be wrong in our lives. Anxiety and discouragement fade away under such focus, and hope and faith arise. So do wisdom, love, joy, and all the other characteristics of Kingdom culture. We begin to flourish when we receive salvation, but we flourish more and more as we grow in it and experience it in all its implications.

This is not intuitive. You will need to be able to see both sides of your salvation—as already certain yet still unfolding. If you see it only as certain, you risk becoming complacent. If you see it only as still unfolding, you risk trying to make sure it happens, under pressure and through performance and pleading. Like the Kingdom of God, it is both "already" and "not yet" here now, but still advancing. On both counts (salvation and the Kingdom of God), let yourself experience it, rest in it, and fully enjoy it.

THE UPWARD CALL

No, dear brothers and sisters, I have not achieved it, but I focus on this one thing: Forgetting the past and looking forward to what lies ahead, I press on to reach the end of the race and receive the heavenly prize for which God, through Christ Jesus, is calling us.

3:13-14

Imagine working tirelessly to preach the gospel to Jews and Gentiles; planting numerous churches and discipling their new believers; putting your life in danger multiple times; being persecuted with beatings, whippings, and stonings; writing letters that will later be considered sacred Scripture; enduring harsh conditions frequently; and being held as a prisoner for several years for the cause—and thinking that's still not enough.

Many of us would be quite satisfied with that level of dedication and fruitfulness, but when we see ourselves as serving someone of infinite value, as Paul did, "enough" never enters the discussion. Paul thought Jesus was worth more than all he had done and wanted to keep pressing ahead. Though he had expressed a readiness to die and be with Christ, he also longed for more fruitfulness (1:21-22). He would pour himself out as long as he could.

That's what Paul referred to as his "calling" toward the "heavenly prize," or, as some translations put it, the "upward call of God in Christ Jesus" (for example, ESV, NKJV). The continuing pursuit not only of Jesus, but of all the gifts and empowerment he endows us with and the works we are privileged to fulfill, leads us ever onward and upward into the joy of his purposes. There is no finish line until we meet him face to face in heaven, and even then our love and joy don't end. Seeing an infinite glory implies unendingly stepping into it.

RE-ENVISION YOUR CALLING

Are you living in an upward call or a downward cycle? This isn't just a matter of semantics. Your outlook will determine your life. God is relentlessly emphatic in Scripture with commands like "do not fear," "be strong and courageous," "only believe," "be filled with hope," and here in Philippians, we repeatedly find the charge to "rejoice." If you see those commands as unattainable ideals, you may feel as if you're spinning your wheels and never getting anywhere. But if you see yourself on an onward and upward journey toward infinite glory—fully endowed with the calling and empowerment to experience it—you keep pressing ahead, not in exhaustion but in wonder and discovery.

Let that be the trajectory of your journey. If it follows the pattern of Jesus (2:6-11), it begins with humility and servanthood, but that is by no means where it ends. The resurrection has already begun for you; you have been raised to new life and can walk in it daily (Romans 6:4). That adventure may entail many challenges, as it did for Paul. But it also involves an ever-ascending growth into the fullness of the Kingdom, experiencing it in greater measure each day.

A FORWARD FOCUS

I focus on this one thing: Forgetting the past and looking forward to what lies ahead, I press on to reach the end of the race.

3:13-14

Paul had a colorful history. He was a Jew from a Hellenized region who was zealous about all things Jewish and eager to reinforce them in his culture—to the point of persecuting people he thought were corrupting it. His vicious pursuit of Christians was a product of his old nature, the consequences of misguided religious beliefs. He mentioned that checkered past from time to time, but he chose not to dwell on it. Like most of us, he had done things he wanted to forget.

But when Paul says he's focusing not on the past but on the future, he isn't just talking about old sins or even his Jewish heritage, with which he began this discussion (3:3-6). He's talking about everything that was over and done.

Many of us tend to be consumed with regret or to second-guess our decisions. We wish we had done some things better, chosen this school or that career, raised our kids with more wisdom, been more intentional with our time, showed people how much we cared, and so on. No matter how true all those regrets may be—and some of them may be quite valid—dwelling on them has little to no benefit and sometimes even perpetuates the consequences of those choices. We can't change what has happened before, but we can influence what is happening now and in the future. Those who live with a purely backward focus miss the present. Those who live in the present can make an enormous difference. The only way to bear the fruit of the Kingdom tomorrow is to cultivate it today.

This is not just a matter of letting bygones be bygones. Our past—in fact, our whole life—is hidden in Christ (see Colossians 3:3). We are wrapped up in him, or as Paul put it a few verses earlier, we are "one with him" (literally, "found in him"; Philippians 3:9). Our old lives were taken with him into the tomb, and we were resurrected with him to live a new life. Old things have passed away, and new things have come (2 Corinthians 5:17). Why would we waste any energy valuing the old life that is now dead and gone? The new—particularly from today going forward—is what matters. (Though there may still be a need to reconcile with someone over past sins.) Paul is not just encouraging his readers to move on because it's psychologically healthy. He is making a profound theological statement about who we are in Christ and how we live as people empowered by his Spirit while pursuing the upward call.

RE-ENVISION YOUR FUTURE

How you see yourself in this journey is vital for how the journey goes. You are currently in ascent, living as a spiritually resurrected bearer of Christ who will one day be physically resurrected too. Everything in this life glistens with newness. It is unhelpful—and quite unbecoming—to dwell in the old.

If you live in regret, understand that those thoughts are not from the Holy Spirit. You are defined by the future God has given you, not the past that happened to you or that you made for yourself. Jesus died to set you free from your past, so why keep going back to it? You are called to live in newness of life, embracing the adventure of being led by the Spirit in ways you've never gone before. Don't waste that opportunity. Everything God has set before you is new. Fix your focus there and walk in it.

GOD STILL SPEAKS

Let all who are spiritually mature agree on these things. If you disagree on some point, I believe God will make it plain to you.

3:15

Human beings have lived in argumentative cultures throughout history. Even from ancient times, political and social commentary—as well as the violence that has often accompanied it—points to a long history of interpersonal complaints. But the vitriol seems to be intensifying in our day, as our virtual connections make hostile commentary immediate and global. Everyone seems to judge everyone else based on whatever seems right in their own eyes, and we have extremely polarized societies as a result. Much of the world is living in attack mode.

Clearly this picture is diametrically opposite of the Kingdom of God, where God is bringing his people together in unity. Yet the world's judgmental ways, with everyone digging in their heels on their own opinions, often infiltrate the church. We cling to our views because, in many cases, we've spent years forming them. We've fit them into what we see as a logical framework, derived from our assumptions about the world, the beliefs we've developed, and the reasoning we've applied. Our perspectives make sense to us.

Most Philippian believers had come to Christ out of a pagan culture because they were convinced of the truth of the gospel. Many of them had seen demonstrations of God's power in the ministry of Paul and his companions (Acts 16) and likely among themselves. But some of them seem to have lost sight of the magnificent obsession that Paul described in the previous verses, perhaps focusing on personal trivialities or prioritizing doctrinal positions over pursuing Jesus himself. They may have been digging in their heels on matters that, in the grand scheme of things, weren't all that important.

Paul saw agreement as a sign of maturity (and implied that if the believers didn't agree, they may not be mature yet). But he also assumed that God would communicate with his people, that Jesus' sheep hear his voice (John 10:27)—an opportunity they may have been neglecting. These believers were not dependent only on Paul's words or their interpretation of Scripture to know the truth or conform to God's nature and purposes. They had access to the Holy Spirit himself. They could listen to him. He would lead them into truth and rearrange their priorities and opinions if they let him.

RE-ENVISION YOUR INTERACTION WITH GOD

We must live with the expectation that God communicates with his people, not just in important matters of direction but also in shaping our beliefs, correcting our misunderstandings, and leading us into greater unity and deeper fellowship. We are not left to figure things out on our own.

The assumptions of many lead them to approach Scripture as merely an ancient document that needs tireless study and interpretation, with the idea that once they know what it says, they know what to do. But Scripture is alive; God still speaks, and members of the fellowship can hear him, let their hearts be changed, and pursue mutual understanding in the Spirit.

If you're mired in a world of conflicting thoughts and ideas—and there are myriads of such thoughts flying around and causing confusion—spend some time seeking the heart of God. Stop and listen to him. Give him time to speak, pausing and worshiping him for a time, and see if his Spirit rises up within you with a leaning one way or another. Take Paul's advice in Philippians 2:1-2 and be drawn together by heart connections rather than intellectual positions. God speaks most often in the context of worshipful hearts and grace-filled relationships. Wisdom *may* come to those who seek answers. It flows freely to those who seek *him*.

LIFTED HIGHER

We must hold on to the progress we have already made.

3:16

Headwinds might seem to present an added challenge for an airplane trying to take off—just one more obstacle to getting a massive piece of machinery in the air—but they actually make it easier. Planes get their lift from the speed of the air passing beneath their wings. What seems like a hindrance is actually a help in getting to greater heights in a shorter amount of time.

The upward call of pursuing the infinite value of knowing Jesus—our spiritual ascent as citizens of heaven—sometimes depends on headwinds. Resistance lifts us to greater heights because it sharpens our focus, cultivates our dependence on the Spirit, and enables us to share in the sufferings of Jesus to some small degree. The Philippian believers had been facing some challenges, but it seems that instead of using those challenges to enhance their spiritual journey and their impact in their community, they had become distracted and disheartened. They may have been letting intimidation and trivialities get in the way of the bigger vision.

The Philippians needed Paul's perspective. The apostle who founded this community of believers could see how far they had come and did not want them to lose the ground they had gained. His message for them to "hold on" to their progress wasn't specific, but we can imagine how they might have interpreted it: *Don't forget what you've already learned. Don't let go of your connection with the Holy Spirit or the words he has spoken to your heart. Don't forfeit your hard-earned reputation in a city filled with things that don't reveal God's heart or reflect his nature. Don't let yourself be distracted.* His words about coming to agreement (3:15) suggest a need to focus on their internal relationships, but as he has indicated at points, the implications are broader. Their internal dynamics have a lot to do with their outward fruit.

RE-ENVISION YOUR ASCENT

We need to understand the dynamics of spiritual entropy—how we are either experiencing that upward call or we aren't. The status quo is not an option in the Kingdom. If we aren't growing, we're losing ground. We may go through seasons that don't look like growth, but as long as we remain in conversation with God in those seasons, the journey is progressing. Passivity and distractions are another matter. Maintaining rarely maintains; it results in disorder and decline, which not only erodes our fellowship but also undermines our impact.

Don't lose heart, give up, or slack off when you encounter life's headwinds, whether from outside the body of Christ or within it. In fact, expand your vision to welcome them. You can use them to your advantage. Accelerate your upward pursuit of knowing Jesus and his infinite worth, and the challenges will lift you higher. A fellowship focused on that singular goal receives healing, begins to thrive, and becomes a testimony to observers. Within and beyond, its members become known as overcomers, their calling becomes much surer, and their "heavenly prize" becomes far more visible.

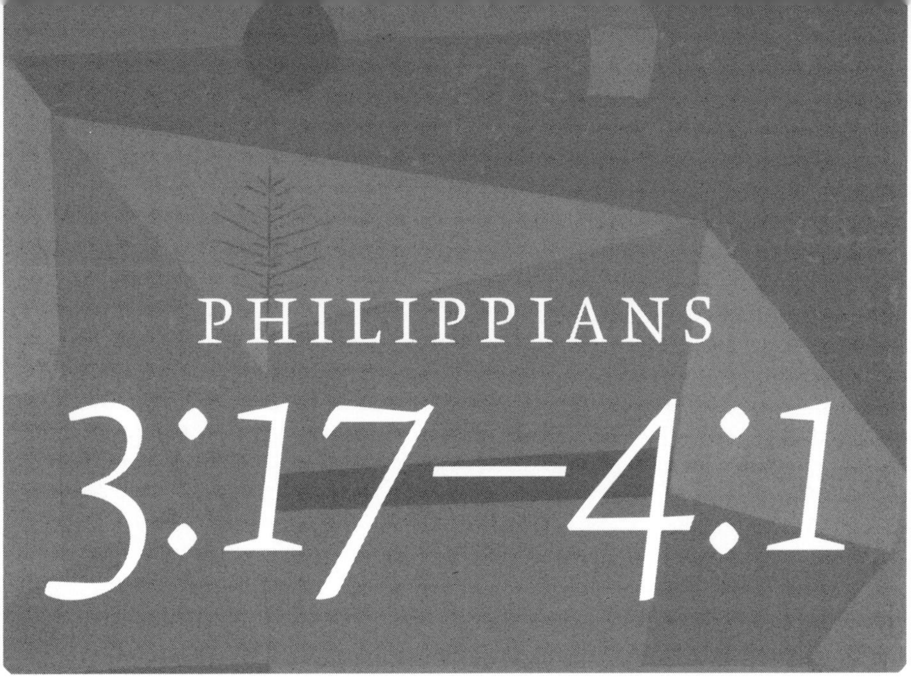

PHILIPPIANS 3:17–4:1

FROM ANOTHER REALM

Paul again refers to himself as an example, this time in the context of his singular pursuit of Jesus and his onward and upward focus on God's Kingdom and the heavenly prize. That pursuit changes how we live on earth. Enemies of the Cross don't grasp the infinite value of knowing Jesus. They even oppose it and turn their hearts and minds to earthly pursuits instead. But we are rooted in another realm. Our King lives in heaven, we seek heavenly treasures, and we focus on our heavenly transformation. As Paul has already pointed out, every knee in every place will bow to him as Lord (2:10). This reality is where we anchor our lives, our hopes, and our expectations.

BACKGROUND

Many Philippians were undoubtedly proud of their Roman-ness, in spite of the Macedonian city's Greek background. Not all residents were citizens, but living in a Roman colony drew them into a sense of imperial significance and enhanced the city's culture and practices in decidedly Roman directions. With the city's military affiliations, its history as the site of a key battle won by Octavian (Caesar Augustus), its meetings and records employing Latin (even as many residents spoke Greek), and its local shrines to the emperor, Philippian civic life exuded loyalty to the imperial center. Yet Paul presented an alternate citizenship, a Lord other than Caesar, and a different culture to live in. Heaven was not like Rome.

THE BIG PICTURE

Citizenship in heaven has huge implications. Just as foreign embassies officially belong to their home country and re-create something of its values and culture, outposts of heaven on earth re-create the values and culture of heaven among the kingdoms of this world. In other words, as Paul has already noted, they should shine the light of heaven into dark places. This means more than just being a good example. It means establishing communities that think, act, and look like their heavenly origins, even reflecting the glories of heaven here on earth for others to see.

Jesus taught his disciples to pray for God's Kingdom to come on earth as it is in heaven. This was never just a prayer for a one-day-in-the-distant-future transformation, and it is certainly not a prayer for believers to escape to heavenly realms while leaving the earth to its own destruction. The Kingdom agenda is for here and now as much as for there and then, and Kingdom citizens have a mission to establish the Kingdom's presence, power, priorities, and precepts as far and wide as we can. One day the King will come and establish it in all its fullness. Until then, we live it out as ambassadors from the eternal realm.

THE MODEL TO FOLLOW

Pattern your lives after mine, and learn from those who follow our example.

3:17

In some sense, the entire letter is summed up in this sentence. From the start, Paul has been modeling a Christian vision, with all its attitudes, perspectives, values, and relational dynamics. He has looked behind the scenes of circumstances to reveal the bigger picture. He has fixed his gaze on eternity and the value of knowing Jesus, while also seeing the present as an opportunity to bear fruit before he meets Jesus face to face. He has demonstrated what a citizen of heaven looks like—joyful, unintimidated, humble, selfless, sacrificial, encouraging, agreeable, uplifting, single-minded, forward-focused, and passionate in pursuit of the infinitely valuable. And he has placed the incarnation, servanthood, death, resurrection, and exaltation of Jesus at the center of it all. He has exemplified what he has been teaching.

The bottom line for the Philippians is that they should learn from the picture Paul has given them—in his life and the lives of those following his example, like Timothy and Epaphroditus. Paul has cast the vision; now it's their turn to step into it. They need to live out what they have seen in him.

That objective is different from simply following instructions. Paul was certainly not afraid to give advice, counsel, and even commands, but he never divorced those imperatives from the big-picture context. He wanted believers to see, feel, and experience Jesus and his Kingdom. Being a disciple was always meant to be more than merely a learning experience. It's a participatory adventure. We don't simply walk after Jesus. We walk with him.

RE-ENVISION YOUR GROWTH

If you have approached following Jesus like reading an instruction manual, recast your vision. God has given you ample pictures and storylines to step into. Any model of discipleship that majors on simply knowledge and application—know the Word, then do the Word—is a truncated version of the gospel and a sure recipe for legalism. Knowing and doing are certainly important, but focusing our efforts there leads to frustration and burnout unless it is backed by vision and the story of God's work in this world. You can't follow Jesus unless you see who he is, as Paul has made so profoundly clear in this letter. You are not just an adherent to biblical principles; you are a participant in the storyline.

Let your vision be captivated by Jesus and those who follow him well. Fill your mind and heart with love for him—who he is and the things he does. Ask him what he thinks, how he feels, what he is doing, and how he wants you to experience him. Look to Paul and others as examples of living by faith and of advancing God's Kingdom in a world that is hostile to it. As you immerse yourself in these images of Jesus, you grow into them. Set your gaze on him and let your heart, your mind, your steps, your desires, your relationships—your everything—follow.

THE TRAGIC CITIZENS

There are many whose conduct shows they are really enemies of the cross of Christ. They are headed for destruction. Their god is their appetite, they brag about shameful things, and they think only about this life here on earth.

3:18-19

We don't know how these citizens of earth in Philippi were causing trouble for its citizens of heaven, but apparently they were. These weren't just people who did the wrong things. They were people who saw incorrectly. Their vision was off. They operated from a false worldview that was shaped by distorted values and the deep wounds every human being has experienced. They were products of a broken world, children of the human rebellion begun so long ago. That's why Paul describes them "with tears in [his] eyes" (3:18). As much as those who opposed Christ might have frustrated and angered the Philippians, their stories were tragic.

The tragic stories continue. The world is still full of people living with distorted vision because of deep spiritual, emotional, and psychological wounds, along with false assumptions and unhealthy coping strategies that come with them. We see this twisted vision in a multitude of expressions: shamelessness, unbridled appetites, unrestrained materialism, brutal judgments, and boastfulness—not only about accomplishments, but also about indecency and selfishness. Such people may not think of themselves as enemies of the cross of Christ—though some openly do—but they demonstrate the exact opposite of the downward-then-upward trajectory of Jesus (2:5-11). Whereas he humbled himself and was exalted, they exalt themselves and will be humbled. We hope they will be humbled in repentance and restoration, but many will ultimately crash on the rocks of their own stubborn ways.

This is why today's ideological arguments rarely sway people from one view to another. The wounds and assumptions go deeper than rational arguments. They are visceral responses to a world of hurt that have often been justified by many complex layers of perceptions and ideas. Coming out from under the systemic deception of the world takes the supernatural presence and power of God, his grace demonstrated through his people, and sometimes years of healing (though God can work remarkably quickly). Even those who are radically following Jesus are still in that process. We are all healing projects in the making.

RE-ENVISION NON-CHRISTIANS

Refuse to envision those who are opposed to the gospel as intellectual opponents who need to be argued into the truth. They are spiritually deceived citizens of a broken world, the dead in need of a resurrection that, in the grand plan of God, is still very possible for each and every one. Pray for them and love them relentlessly, even as you guard yourself against their harmful words and ways. God does not lose hope for anyone. Neither should you. In fact, the lives of healed, transformed believers are the greatest testimony of hope for a world of hurting people. See yourself on solid ground, even if all the world shifts around you, and live with compassion for those who are desperately, even aggressively, embracing lies as they grasp for truth.

WHERE YOU RESIDE

We are citizens of heaven, where the Lord Jesus Christ lives.

3:20

Paul did not take on a Roman identity, but he did rely on his Roman citizenship when it was useful to him. One of those situations was his first visit to Philippi, when he and Silas were beaten and imprisoned and then miraculously delivered. Paul refused to leave without holding city officials accountable for their unlawful treatment of Roman citizens (Acts 16:16-40). Another was Paul's appeal to Caesar while under arrest in Jerusalem, which prompted his journey to Rome and the confinement during which he wrote this letter (Acts 25:1-12). Paul understood matters of identity and citizenship, yet he subordinated both his Jewish identity (see Philippians 3:5-9) and his Roman privileges for a much higher status. Above all, he was a citizen of heaven.

All believers are. Just as Paul's Roman citizenship gave him access to the privileges of Rome, his primary citizenship—and ours—provides access to the privileges of heaven. In a spiritual—but very real—sense, we live where Jesus lives. Through him, we have access to the resources he has. We are not simply citizens of earth trying to access heaven and praying that heaven's blessings come down; we have authority and status in heaven to distribute its resources on earth. These prayers may sound the same, but the mind and heart behind them are entirely different. If we realize we are already seated in the heavenly realms (see Ephesians 2:6), we think, live, pray, and relate to others with confidence. We become filled with faith because we know who we are.

Because citizens of heaven reproduce the environment of heaven wherever they are, consider the environment around you. Are you creating a culture of love, joy, peace, faith, hope, encouragement, affirmation, assurance, interdependence, and truth? Or a culture of self-effort, self-sufficiency, insecurity, stress, fear, disapproval, and judgment? Do people feel alive around you? Do they sense the Kingdom you are carrying within you? The answers to those questions will tell you a lot about how thoroughly rooted you are in your heavenly citizenship.

RE-ENVISION YOUR HOME COUNTRY

Become aware of where you mentally reside. You see the world all around you, and since you grew up here, you instinctively think of it as your home country. But something shifted when you believed. Your primary citizenship was transferred to another realm, even while you continued to live very consciously in this one. You are now essentially an expat in a foreign land (see 1 Peter 2:11)—one that ideally is becoming even more foreign to you as you pursue that upward call. Though the tangible, fallen world is still right in front of you, you are to keep seeking the things above, setting your sights on the realities of heaven (Colossians 3:1), walking by faith and not by sight (2 Corinthians 5:7). The big picture of heavenly citizenship is meant to capture your heart and mind and shape your entire experience.

If it doesn't, you risk being drawn off course with mixed loyalties, misplaced values, and the demands and urgencies of what you see around you. Your spirit feels stuck on earth rather than soaring above it. But if you immerse yourself in your identity as a citizen of heaven, envisioning yourself as seated in that realm even as you walk on earth, your perspective, faith, prayers, relationships, and sense of mission change. You live out your calling with power. And your life—and your world—begins to look a lot more heavenly.

A LIFE-ALTERING PARADIGM

We are eagerly waiting for him to return as our Savior. He will take our weak mortal bodies and change them into glorious bodies like his own, using the same power with which he will bring everything under his control.

3:20-21

Paul earlier presented a vision of who Jesus is: the one who relinquished divine privileges to become a man, served humanity by dying on our behalf, and was exalted above every name. Now he presents a vision of who we are: those who humble themselves, who serve each other, and who will be raised to glory, living where Jesus is as citizens of the heavenly realm, having followed the divine trajectory to the end. When we live with that end in mind, all of Paul's instructions about living with humility as servants of each other, along with his commands about living without anxiety and fear, become much more doable. We grow toward the visions we've placed in our hearts, and we make sacrifices knowing that the coming glory far outweighs their costs. Our eager expectation of Jesus' return profoundly influences our attitudes and actions today.

If you really begin to see yourself as a citizen of heaven—not just knowing that identity as a theological truth but living as though it's the core of who you are—the trajectory of your life becomes fundamentally driven by that reality. And if you are absolutely convinced that your weak mortal body will be transformed by the unfathomable power of God—the same power that created the world and raised Jesus out of death—you begin to live without fear. The strategies the rest of the world desperately use in order to grab as much life as they can are no longer necessary for you. The mantra "You only live once" hardly has an effect on someone whose *once* includes a glorious eternity filled with heaven's blessings. You are free to live as someone who has nothing to lose and has already gained everything.

That's why Paul was able to talk about his life-or-death situation as a win-win proposition (1:20-24). It's also why Jesus freely gave up the privileges of deity for a time, and why Timothy and Epaphroditus followed Paul's example in pouring out their lives for the cause. No humility of service or humiliation of the Cross is the end of the story for a person whose gaze is fixed on eternity. An infinite future lies open before us.

RE-ENVISION ETERNITY

This reorientation is an enormous paradigm shift for any human being. Paul's words are not a consolation prize for those who are suffering or a pat on the back for the discouraged. They are life-altering. We are like ants emerging over the edge of a small rock to suddenly see the enormity of the Grand Canyon. We thought our journey was filled with bumps and crevices, but now it is filled with vast universes both seen and unseen. And we are promised an astonishing position at the throne of one who has gone before and rules over all. Nothing is left to fear or dread. All of heaven's glories are set before us.

CROWNS OF FAITHFULNESS

Therefore, my dear brothers and sisters, stay true to the Lord. I love you and long to see you, dear friends, for you are my joy and the crown I receive for my work.

4:1

Paul envisioned a crown. He was not expecting kingship, though he likely would have agreed with Peter's picture of believers as a royal priesthood, kings and queens and priests in God's realm. But he understood that our eternal destiny is shaped by this brief moment in time when we are able to bear Kingdom fruit in a barren world. So he was willing and eager to remain in the flesh for the sake of the Philippians (1:23-25). More time in this life expanded that window of opportunity. With the grand vista of eternity open before him, he sought to bring certain manifestations of the Kingdom into that eternity with him. The Philippians were one of those manifestations.

In light of the compelling, paradigm-shifting vision of heavenly citizenship Paul has already presented, the Philippians should find it easier to "stay true to the Lord." Earlier, Paul had suggested that, in some sense, his crown was contingent on their faithfulness (2:16), but here (as in 1:6), he seems entirely confident that their story will end well. One of the reasons for that is a renewed vision, which he has stoked again and again in this letter. An uncertain future makes for an uncertain present—doubts, insecurities, anxieties, fears, and petty conflicts about momentary matters. But a future that is certain changes everything. It frees us to live with abandon, casting all our hopes on the one who secured that future for us. And it motivates us to work while we can (John 9:4), making the most of every opportunity (Ephesians 5:16), knowing that fruitfulness increases with age (Philippians 1:25). Our work is an investment in eternity, and the interest never stops compounding.

RE-ENVISION YOUR JOURNEY

By definition, grace is unearned. But the idea of believers receiving rewards for their faithfulness and fruitfulness is thoroughly embedded in the teachings of Jesus and New Testament writers. Paul saw the Philippians as a crown, a laurel around his head, a feather in his cap, a validation of his ministry that would stand in eternity. We, too, are to see our lives as windows of opportunity for fruitfulness, sowing seeds that only God can make grow, cultivating faithfulness that he fully intends to reward. God gives us glimpses of our fruitfulness in the here and now, but we won't see its full effects until we live more completely in the realm of our citizenship. Our sight will become much clearer when our bodies are transformed.

In the meantime, we are to fill our spiritual eyes with God's ever-expanding Kingdom on earth. We are never told to focus on how bad things are or how much evil is in the world, even as we remain aware of it. Instead, we focus on what God is doing and what he has called us to do. We stay true, choose to rejoice, fix our gaze on eternity, and bear fruit that will last. We pursue the infinite value of knowing Jesus as our ultimate reward, even while being crowned now and forever with the fruits of our labor. Our future vision brings the culture of the Kingdom into our present days and fills them with joy.

PHILIPPIANS 4:2-9

A NEW, TRUE PERSPECTIVE

At several points, Paul has referred indirectly to disagreements, complaints, and self-interests. Now he gets more specific. Two women of influence within the church are at odds with each other, and he appeals to them to settle their differences. But he also takes the opportunity to address everyone's attitudes. Peace is not just a matter of eliminating discord within the fellowship. It also involves filling the hearts of its members with joy, gratitude, and thoughts that align with the truth and goodness of the God of peace. Hearts and minds overflowing with Kingdom values and affections have no room for discord and worry. People focused on a big God—like Paul in his pursuit of the infinite value of knowing Jesus—are not pulled off course with smaller details.

BACKGROUND

Euodia and Syntyche had worked with Paul and others to spread the Good News, advance the Kingdom, and establish the church in Philippi. At some point a disagreement arose between these two women. We don't know if it was a personality conflict, a doctrinal issue, or a practical matter, but it may have drawn others into taking sides, potentially splitting the fellowship. Whatever it was, it wasn't important enough to Paul for him to rebuke either one of them. He was certainly willing to enter conflict when the stakes were high—as in 3:2, where the gospel was being compromised—but he wasn't engaging in this dispute. He wanted them all to remember their affection for each other and to come to agreement (see 2:1-4).

Paul appealed to his "true partner" to help (4:3). No one knows who this person was—speculation includes Luke, Lydia, and various other possibilities—but he or she was evidently a trusted leader in the church. So was Clement, about whom we also know no details. But we learn through all these references that leadership was distributed among several people, including women, and Paul was willing to rely on those who had worked with him in the past. He entrusted the mission to faithful partners.

THE BIG PICTURE

This passage (along with many others) affirms that the Bible teaches us to think very positively according to truth. Despite Paul's implicit concern regarding the discord in the Philippian church, this passage is filled with hope and joy. He offers instructions to think in new, good, true ways. Scripture tells us to convince ourselves of things that are true, and the truth of our salvation is wonderfully positive and full of hope. It gives us an extraordinary new identity, births us into an entirely new creation, and is accompanied by astonishingly good promises. God's Word repeatedly presents a picture of who we really are, the beauty of the new creation, the extravagant gifts he has given us, and the glorious inheritance we are receiving. Through and through, the message is good news for those who believe and serves to counter discord.

Most of what Paul instructs in this section cannot be carried out by people looking from an earthly perspective toward heaven rather than a heavenly perspective toward earth. Those who see themselves as rooted in this world, even as they long for another, have a hard time rising above their immediate concerns. But that's Paul's point here: Many of the Philippians' problems are a matter of perspective. No matter how real the issues are, they look too big when those involved have a vision that isn't filled with God and his goodness. Only in light of an overwhelming, intimate relationship with the one of infinite value—a "knowledge" available only to citizens of heaven (see 3:8)—do the mountains of human experience turn into manageable little mounds. And only in that light do our worries and troubling thoughts turn into joy, gratitude, and peace.

I appeal to Euodia and Syntyche. Please, because you belong to the Lord, settle your disagreement. And I ask you, my true partner, to help these two women, for they worked hard with me in telling others the Good News. They worked along with Clement and the rest of my co-workers, whose names are written in the Book of Life.

4:2-3

In light of all Paul has written—his vision of God working in every situation for good, the pattern of humility Jesus demonstrated, the world's destiny of every knee bowing before Jesus, and our personal destiny as citizens of heaven whose bodies will be transformed—the conflict between Euodia and Syntyche, and any related factionalism, seems quite small. Paul chooses not to take sides in their dispute, perhaps to demonstrate the infinite value of a singular pursuit of knowing Jesus. Also, he has already urged all the Philippian believers to work together in one mind and purpose (2:1-3). Their conflict does not fit the Kingdom culture he is promoting. Most conflicts don't.

Most conflicts occur in the context of small-picture visions, where people are driven by their own limited agendas and self-interests. A big-picture vision of the Kingdom usually makes those concerns seem superfluous, much like a huge crisis or swell of patriotism brings together people of a nation who would normally not associate with each other. Paul was willing to lay down his life for a greater glory. He had a strong vision of what brings life and what doesn't. Whatever these women were arguing about, it wasn't breathing life into the fellowship. It needed to fade away under the light of a much brighter purpose.

RE-ENVISION THE KINGDOM ENVIRONMENT

If you truly catch a vision of the Kingdom and the environment it brings—truth, beauty, love, order, harmony, and the free flow of Kingdom life—carrying out that vision becomes a willing sacrifice, not a burdensome chore. If you see joy and peace as priorities over being right or having your way, you begin pursuing them and cast aside anything that gets in the way. You become eager to lay down differences both to cultivate and to enjoy the atmosphere of the Kingdom around you.

This Kingdom environment is available to anyone who wants it. It's there for the taking right now. But it doesn't just happen. It comes at a cost. We want to experience the Kingdom on our own terms, with our agenda included in it, so we often unwittingly prioritize contentiousness over peace. In other words, we live in our small stories more than the bigger one. We miss out on the beauty and glory of Kingdom fellowship, often because people simply rub us the wrong way.

Lift your eyes above the fray. Refuse to play in the shallows when you can step into the depths of God's rivers of grace. Submit your personal agenda to God's much bigger one—which, by the way, he is fully able to accomplish. Choose the flow of the Spirit and all that comes with it. The environment of the Kingdom is always a much more pleasant experience than a contest of human wills.

Always be full of joy. . . . Let everyone see. . . . Remember. . . . Don't worry . . . pray. . . . Tell God . . . thank him. . . . Fix your thoughts. . . . Think about things. Keep putting into practice. . . .

4:4-6, 8-9

The human heart projects whatever is inside it to the outside world. That's why you can walk into a room of people and feel energized, deflated, encouraged, nervous, or any other sense within the range of human emotions. The people there have set the atmosphere with their anticipation, fears, hopes, anger, and so on. In other words, emotions are contagious, and our inner workings have quite a significant effect. And those inner workings generally reflect whatever we've fixed our minds on.

Philippians 4:1-9 represents Paul's effort to shift this congregation from being issue-minded people to being vision-minded people. It's human nature to focus on issues—problems, needs, complicated situations, potential threats—and the Philippians seem to have been doing so on several fronts. But an issue-oriented life is never at peace, because it always has something to fix. So Paul tries to direct them away from whatever issues confront them, looking instead toward the environment of their hearts, the culture within them, the character of the Kingdom and how it would play out in their fellowship and in their larger world. An issue-shaped heart projects its burdens, anxieties, discouragement, stress, and more into its environment. A heaven-shaped heart projects the characteristics of the Kingdom. Paul knows these believers will influence their fellowship and their world with whatever is in them, and what's in them isn't necessarily helpful.

This is particularly true with regard to worry and the lack of joy it entails. When we worry, we devote our faith to our problems. We empower them—not only in our own minds but also in our experience. Since the things we focus on grow stronger, we must stop paying attention to unhelpful things. It is far better to focus on the environment in our hearts, which inevitably plays out in our lives, rather than on issues.

This does not mean we should avoid issues. We will have to deal with them. But we cannot afford to deal with them without having the right heart and mindset. If our faith changes the world, and if the faith that is in us is being devoted to problems and empowering them, we are not changing the world the way we want to. We may even be reinforcing a climate of hopelessness.

RE-ENVISION YOUR ISSUES

Learn to see your heart and mind as world-influencers—not some mysterious vibe or energy, but as places where world-changing faith is cultivated. Whatever does not stir up faith is contrary to heaven's perspective and is changing the world negatively. It also becomes a burden you were never meant to carry. Every concern that comes to mind should be a prompt for prayer, not an occasion to mull something over apart from God. The concern may remain, but the weight of it is on him. That's why Paul urges joy, gratitude, prayer, and good and true thoughts so insistently in this passage. The Philippians had the power to change their world from the inside out, if they would grasp the connection between their inner and outer lives. You do too.

IMPERATIVE JOY

Always be full of joy in the Lord. I say it again—rejoice!

4:4

This verse contains the fourth and fifth instances when Paul has told the Philippians to rejoice (2:17-18; 3:1). He has also mentioned his own joy again and again (1:4, 18; 2:17-18; 4:1). The thought of these believers filled him with joy—he obviously had a lot of affection for them—but infusing this letter with the theme of joy reflects more than an overflow of his feelings. He was intentionally modeling joy and telling the believers that they needed it. Joy is a vital, non-negotiable aspect of the Christian life.

We may read these words as merely happy encouragement from a friend, but joy is a necessary aspect of a believer's well-being. Paul commands believers to have it, and we must insist on it and persevere in it. And here Paul makes it clear that joy is not just an attitude to embrace from time to time. We are to rejoice *always*. In everything. Along with gratitude and prayer—Paul explicitly links these three themes not only in 4:4-6 but also in Philippians 1:3-4 and 1 Thessalonians 5:16-18—joy reorients our lives completely.

People who are filled with joy—and it is a choice, or at least something we can choose to cultivate by focusing on what's true, honorable, right, pure, lovely, and admirable (Philippians 4:8)—generally aren't interested in nitpicking and aren't dismayed by opposition or setbacks. Their joy consumes their problems. They may experience grief and righteous anger, but they won't be overcome by it. Their big preoccupation overshadows their lesser preoccupations. They live in, and rejoice in, the big picture.

Paul demonstrates this perspective when he rejoices that the gospel is being preached, even by people with selfish motives (1:18). He is offering more than encouragement and takes aim at the very root of what the Philippians are dealing with. If they would change their focus and embrace the kind of joy Paul has, much of what they are dealing with would fade away.

If you've ever tried to stir up supernatural joy, you know how impossible it is without a heaven-to-earth view. If you see yourself as rooted on earth, seeking a very occasional taste of heaven, joy will be sporadic, always punctuated with the urgencies and contingencies of life. But if you know you're seated in heaven—that you're an unshakable, unassailable citizen of another realm—and look at life on earth from that perspective, you can be filled with constant joy. After all, joy is the climate of the Kingdom. Or, as C. S. Lewis put it, it's "the serious business of Heaven."* This is how Kingdom citizens see the world.

That may take some retraining—Paul will get to that in 4:8—because of the well-established neural pathways in our minds. Those old thought patterns keep us from having to relearn everything every day, but they can also make new thought patterns difficult. That's why re-envisioning is so important. Seeing all of life in a new way makes learning new ways of thinking much more natural and possible.

RE-ENVISION YOUR JOY

Learn to see joy not only as an option but also as an imperative. A lifestyle of joyful worship and gratitude does wonders for our trivial annoyances. And in the grand scheme of things, most of our annoyances are trivial. Joy keeps them from coming to the forefront of our minds, where they don't need to be, and begins that process of retraining our minds on the right things. When we've filled our minds with something much bigger and better and worthwhile—when we choose to focus on the big story—the little stories can't eat away at us. We live in the expansiveness of God's Kingdom rather than the narrowness of our world. And the narrowness of our world loses any power it once held over our lives.

---

* C. S. Lewis, *Letters to Malcolm: Chiefly on Prayer* (San Diego: Harvest, 1964), 93.

Let everyone see that you are considerate in all you do. Remember, the Lord is coming soon.

4:5

"The Lord is coming soon" is literally rendered "the Lord is near," which has multiple implications. It can mean that the Lord is near in proximity—that he is present with us, imparting his humility, joy, and outlook through his Spirit. When people realize that the same Jesus who humbled himself and then was exalted is present, attitudes change.

It can also mean that the Lord is near chronologically—that his return is near on the timeline, making mundane concerns and conflicts irrelevant. When people realize that the same Lord whom every tongue will honor and before whom every knee will bow is ready to return, priorities change.

Either way, his nearness makes everything look different. Paul's instructions carry more weight, whether in Jesus' close presence or his imminent return. A focus on Jesus heals relationships, increases joy, unravels our anxieties, and as in this verse, provokes more kindness, gentleness, and consideration toward others. The whole package of attitudes in this section of the letter is important for the fellowship and for their witness to the world. Paul knew the Kingdom would spread through communities of believers. The perspectives, attitudes, and relational dynamics that characterize those communities is paramount.

The Kingdom still spreads through communities of believers, and what those communities look like still matters. Paul knew from hard experience that sour relationships with the city could bring marginalization or even oppression, threatening Christians' peaceful existence. He also knew that when God's Spirit transforms a community, that community can transform the culture around it. A move of the Spirit through his people can change the spiritual climate of a city and prepare for Kingdom growth. But it begins with believers demonstrating the kindness of God.

RE-ENVISION YOUR WITNESS

If you see the church's mission as a matter only of speaking truth to the world, you'll go forth with a message. Many have done so, but they have carried that message in the wrong spirit—with judgment, disapproval, condescension, or pressure. But if you see the church's mission as a matter of embodying the nature of God and his Kingdom, you'll go forth with a demonstration. That demonstration includes speaking truth, but it puts truth in context. It reveals God's heart and empowers the message. Words of truth alone don't spread the Kingdom culture. Demonstrations of truth do.

What happens when a community of believers embodies the character and nature of God? The kingdom of darkness feels threatened and may provoke some resistance, but more importantly, people are drawn to the Father's love and kindness, which leads to repentance (Romans 2:4). They are captivated by a picture of what healthy relationships can look like. And whether they realize it or not, they sense his presence. The Lord is near not only *to* his people; he is also near *through* them.

BEYOND ANXIETY

Don't worry about anything.

4:6

Apparently the Philippians were worried. We don't know why, though Paul has given plenty of hints throughout the letter of some external and internal pressures. Were they experiencing rejection and oppression from city authorities? If so, Paul's words about displaying consideration for everyone to see (4:5) might be intended to ease the tension. It would also explain why they might be anxious. After all, Paul had found Philippi to be a hostile environment on his first visit there. That hostility may well have carried over to the Christian community in the following years.

Yet Paul's words are more sweeping than simply not being anxious about opposition. He says not to be anxious about *anything*. We can take that as broadly as we want to. In no area of life does God tells us, "Maybe you should be anxious about this. It's out of my hands." Anxiety is a common human experience, but nowhere in Scripture does God validate it as something we should just accept. In fact, just the opposite. He repeatedly tells his people to trust him, believe his promises, rest in his care, and reject fear. When we worry, we are at some level questioning his wisdom, power, or love. Genuine, heartfelt faith and basking in his overwhelming love can eliminate those fears.

God wouldn't tell us not to worry if we had legitimate reasons to do so.

Therefore we don't have such reasons. His instructions through Paul are not just about easing our minds; they are about nurturing the Kingdom culture within us. The environment inside us tends to shape the environment outside us, and worry is not worth reproducing. It makes for a poor testimony to the world around us. God is interested in our own peace of mind, but he is also interested in having his people display his nature for all to see. If Jesus is truly near, as Paul wrote in the previous verse, his nearness should be evident in our peaceful state.

RE-ENVISION YOUR ANXIETY

Like joy in the midst of adverse circumstances, peace cannot reign in our hearts unless we look at life from a heaven-to-earth perspective. From our position in that higher realm, where our confidence in God's ability and willingness to answer prayer is strong, earth's problems are clearly no match for him. From an earth-to-heaven perspective, we aren't so sure. Our vision gets muddied. We let our problems—or even just potential problems—look bigger than God.

Continue to situate yourself in heavenly realms, seeing your life and this world from that perspective, recognizing all that is going on beyond our immediate, visible surroundings. Read between the lines of circumstances to see God at work; believe in his goodness and live with the expectation that you will see it in this life and the next; and let every area of your life radiate hope. This is God's will for you, and his promises put it in writing. God dwells high above our worries. He wants us to dwell there with him too.

THE ENVIRONMENT OF PRAYER

Instead, pray about everything. Tell God what you need, and thank him for all he has done.

4:6

Years earlier, Paul wrote to the church at Thessalonica and told them very succinctly, "Always be joyful. Never stop praying. Be thankful in all circumstances" (1 Thessalonians 5:16-18). At the beginning of his letter to the Philippians, he wrote that he was thankful to God for this church and that he prayed for them with joy (Philippians 1:3-4). So when Paul gives instructions here to pray and thank God, in the context of being joyful (4:4), he is reiterating a common theme. Joy, prayer, and gratitude work together. They all contribute to and flow out of a Kingdom environment and the hearts that immerse themselves in it.

This combination of joy, gratitude, and prayer is foundational. Prayers rooted in desperation or anxiety are not as powerful as prayers rooted in confident faith. They don't catch the spirit of the Kingdom. God often honors and answers them because he hears our cries and cares about the needs and desires of our hearts. But prayer that is rooted in the culture of the Kingdom is not tinged with desperation or fear. It's filled with faith and hope. And faith and hope cannot thrive outside of a context of joy and gratitude.

A literal translation of this verse integrates thanksgiving into the prayer itself—not only for what God has already done but also for what he is doing and is going to do. If we really believe God is going to answer our prayers, we can go ahead and thank him for the answers, whatever they happen to be. Having gratitude that he hears and will respond reflects faith and stirs hope, filling our prayers with confidence and expectation. That anticipation, rooted in joy, powerfully displays the culture of the Kingdom and honors the love, power, and purposes of God.

RE-ENVISION YOUR PRAYERS

Do you think of your prayers as requests that might get answered or as communication that God is already invested in? Are God's promises tangible enough for you to bank on? Is your heart at rest when you present your requests to him or anxious that those requests may not do any good? Are you able to thank him for however he will respond, whether or not his response is exactly what you expect? If not, you may need a different vision of prayer.

Prayer is not a shot in the dark that may or may not hit its target. It may seem like a desperate plea at times, but that should be the exception. In every case, prayer should flow out of a relationship that is filled with warmth, intimacy, joy, gratitude, and anticipation—and it can be infused with celebration from the start, even if the outcome still seems up in the air. It would not be unreasonable to infuse your prayers with some dancing and shouting from the start, because one way or another, they will end in some kind of victory. You are praying to a God who is on your side (see Romans 8:31), just as you are on his. You aren't negotiating with him across the table; he is sitting next to you as your advocate. Celebrate that fact every time you pray, look forward to whatever awesome thing he is going to do, and let your heart be at peace.

TRANSCENDENT PEACE

Then you will experience God's peace, which exceeds anything we can understand. His peace will guard your hearts and minds as you live in Christ Jesus.

4:7

Jesus never panicked. He did not let the disciples or anyone else rush him, and he was not consumed with worry. He even slept in the midst of a raging storm. He prayed intensely as the Cross loomed, and his heart was troubled for a time, but he resolutely fixed his gaze on the joy awaiting him and pressed ahead with certainty (Hebrews 12:2). Whether immediately or eventually, he approached every situation with stillness in his soul.

That peace is available to us too. It may take a radical reorientation of our perspective and thought patterns to receive it, but we can. In this verse, Paul shows us how.

The Philippians were apparently anxious, and Paul told them not to worry. In fact, he gave them an antidote to worry. They could replace those anxious thoughts with prayer—not just any kind of prayer, but prayer that is saturated in joy and gratitude, where faith and hope grow strong. Minds and hearts steeped in those attributes grow immune to disruptive concerns because they are anchored in a higher, deeper reality known only to citizens of heaven. In fact, joyful, grateful prayer shifts the spiritual environment within us from turmoil to transcendence, lifting us above oppressive concerns and into the throne room of God, where peace and power reign. We begin to see things differently in that place. We don't have to understand how God is going to work things out; we just know he will. What once seemed huge and intimidating becomes minor and manageable. We begin to expect miracles. And our hearts are filled with peace.

RE-ENVISION YOUR HEART

The best way to arrive at this peace is to cultivate a heart of worship, joy, and gratitude. Most people tend to see their concerns as big and God as small because their concerns dominate their vision while God appears far away. It's a rather convincing vision, even when we know it isn't true. But a lifestyle of worship exposes that illusion and restores a hopeful perspective. When God dominates our vision, everything else—every threat, problem, and setback—appears powerless. Praise-saturated hearts are fertile soil for faith, and worries wither away.

Don't let your anxious thoughts simmer. That will only intensify the anxiety. Instead, use those concerns as prayer prompts. Turn your worries into prayer requests that are filled with joyful anticipation that God is taking care of them. You'll need to persist—anxious thoughts can be relentless—but eventually peace settles in. When our prayers and gratitude bring us into a place of expectancy, we stop wondering whether God will intervene and start imagining all the ways he could. Sometimes we can just pull up a chair and watch him work, firmly convinced we'll be amazed by his creativity. No problem can compete with his solutions, and no concern can compete with his peace.

Fix your thoughts on what is true, and honorable, and right, and pure, and lovely, and admirable. Think about things that are excellent and worthy of praise.

4:8

Our inner and outer worlds are profoundly, mysteriously connected in myriad ways. The relationships we develop, the attitudes we carry, the decisions we make, the activities we pursue, the work we do, and the habits we practice determine the course of our lives and affect many people around us. These outer lives shape our inner selves, but our inner lives feed our outer lives even more. Whatever is going on inside us is often reproduced outside.

That's why cultivating a Kingdom environment within—in our thoughts, feelings, intentions, and perceptions—has everything to do with extending the Kingdom culture out into our world. Many people see themselves as victims of their own thought processes, but we have control over what we think and see. So Paul instructs the Philippians to dwell on whatever fits the Kingdom. Our minds are to become thoroughly preoccupied with the Kingdom's truths, values, characteristics, purposes, and beauty, which means they are also thoroughly unoccupied with contentiousness, worry, fear, misplaced priorities, selfish agendas, and anything else that does not represent the Kingdom or exemplify its culture. We simply cannot afford to have thoughts swirling in our minds that do not align with God's. Such thoughts inevitably lead us away from him and undermine our faith. They are antagonists to the fruit of the Spirit. We have to let our minds be renewed and transformed (see Romans 12:2).

That's a challenge. Like trickles that turn into streams that turn into rivers rushing down a mountainside, our neural pathways become more deeply entrenched over time. Old thought patterns literally defend themselves against new patterns, which is why our resolutions are so hard to follow through on and why well-worn anxieties are so hard to overcome. Rerouting our thoughts requires relentless persistence, a clear vision, and inspiration from the Holy Spirit. It also requires the practice of replacement. We can't just get rid of old thoughts; we have to replace them with new ones.

That's Paul's instruction in this verse. These are the substitutes for old ways of thinking. These new preoccupations undo our worries, cultivate joy, open our eyes to what God is doing even in adverse circumstances, and cause us to live like citizens of heaven and shine as lights in a dark world. They empower us to refuse to be intimidated, value the fellowship and serve each other, and root our prayers in faith and gratitude. In other words, these ways of thinking enable us to do what Paul has been teaching throughout the course of this letter. Renewed minds become saturated in Kingdom ways.

RE-ENVISION YOUR THOUGHT LIFE

Be careful about where your mind goes. To cultivate a Kingdom environment within that creates Kingdom experiences without, fix your vision on what the Kingdom looks like: love, truth, beauty, order, peace, joy, and whatever else gives life and fills the heart with meaning, purpose, and celebration. Soak in that vision. Cultivate it daily. See it not only in eternity but also in the here and now. Imagine what this world would look like if it were saturated in a Kingdom environment, then exclude from your thoughts whatever doesn't fit that picture. Whatever disrupts, distracts from, or distorts that image in your life, let it go. Fill your life with whatever is excellent and worthy of praise.

A LIFE OF PEACE

Keep putting into practice all you learned and received from me—everything you heard from me and saw me doing. Then the God of peace will be with you.

4:9

It's one thing to hear the truth. It's another to see it at work in someone's life. Lessons are better caught than taught, which is why God gave us a Bible full of life stories, visual images, dramatic examples, and real situations. We *see* the Kingdom at work in his Word. For example, instead of simply being told that God is good to us, we're given memorable pictures of the Lord as our Shepherd or the Deliverer who guides us through deep waters. These images stir our expectations that he will do for us what he has done for others. We learn to live with a vision of who he is and what his Kingdom is like.

Paul reminds the Philippians that everything he has been teaching has been demonstrated in his own life. This is not the first time he has pointed to himself as an example; he was quite explicit about it in 3:17. But in case they missed it or didn't realize how important his demonstration was, he tells them again. He has seen God at work even in situations that look like adversity and fixed his gaze on eternity and fruitfulness rather than the details about his own life and death. He has cast the Philippians' opposition as powerless and self-destructive, foregrounded the example of Jesus as their pattern for humility and exaltation, and seen the believers as lights that shine in darkness rather than being lost in it. He has positioned God's people as citizens of heaven rather than of Rome, demonstrated unbridled joy in everything and no anxiety about anything, prayed with gratitude, and steeped his thoughts in the culture of the Kingdom All of this forms a case study in Kingdom life and attitudes.

But Paul's repetition on the theme comes with an addition here. This pattern of his, which he has amply described and exemplified, is the life that leads to peace. Some of his audience might have questioned that statement. Paul had experienced a lot of things that weren't peaceful at all, including his first visit to Philippi, which resulted in a brutal beating with rods, painful chains, and an awkward exit from the city. But Paul was referring to a different kind of peace—the kind that is able to see through all the turmoil and hardship and embrace the bigger picture. In spite of all that had happened to him, Paul's heart was at rest. The entirety of this letter explains why.

RE-ENVISION PEACE

Most people live with an "if only" hope. If only they had a better job, a higher income, a different home, a new location, a fresh start, a fulfilling relationship, then life would be great. But that never leads to peace. It results in a constant search for ideal situations—in other words, unending restlessness.

The God of peace offers something much better: a life above the fray—not avoiding it or ignoring it but seeing through it and ministering in the midst of it from a position of strength. In this vision of peace, God works with the believer through the things of heaven to influence matters on earth. There is no restlessness there, only still souls with clear vision and unwavering hope. That's peace, and there's no "if only" about it.

PHILIPPIANS 4:10-23

ALWAYS ENOUGH—AND MORE

Paul began this letter with joy and gratitude for the Philippian church, acknowledging them as partners in the gospel. Here he repeats much the same message. One reason Paul wrote this letter, among others, was to express appreciation for their gift. But this was not merely a thank-you note recognizing receipt of the gift. The entire focus is relational, not transactional. In fact, he never explicitly says "thank you." He affirms their partnership, expresses joy, talks about their bonds of friendship, pours out advice, and encourages them—with an emphatic reminder that all their provision, material and otherwise, flows from God's riches in glory.

BACKGROUND

The churches of Macedonia were generally not well off (2 Corinthians 8:1-3), which may explain why the Philippians had not helped Paul in a while

(Philippians 4:10). But they had given what they could on more than one occasion (4:15-16). Paul knew they had made a sacrifice—evidence that they already understood something of the servant-heartedness he had written about so eloquently and asked them to apply to each other—and he valued that gift highly, especially for the heart behind it.

The giving and receiving of gifts in Greek and Roman societies was surrounded by complex social conventions. Gifts were statements that came with expectations and questions. Was the giver making a statement about his or her status by providing for someone in need? Would the receiver reciprocate—and assert his or her status by the amount—or remain obligated and subordinate to the giver? Did the transaction bind the parties together in a patron-client relationship, with implications for future interactions? Transactions were loaded with nuances of meaning.

Paul navigated his gratitude by avoiding the language of obligation—on both sides of the relationship. The closest he comes to reciprocating their gift is a promise that God would provide for them out of his infinite resources. That's a much better offer than Paul returning a favor out of his own resources. The Philippians could rest in God's continuing care.

THE BIG PICTURE

In keeping with his pattern of seeing circumstances as opportunities, Paul recognized that his need led to an occasion for the Philippians' generosity. He was not at all worried that they would suffer lack—especially since he had just told them not to worry about anything (4:6)—or that his own needs would not be met, whether by them or some other means. In fact, he saw every situation of need as God's opportunity to be generous. One way or another, God would provide.

When we view our resources as simply finite, every loss or expense is a cause for concern. It subtracts from what we have. But when we view our resources as infinite—they come from the storehouse of an infinite God, after all—every loss or expense is a cause for joy. God will compensate for the loss by adding to what we have in one form or another. One perspective begins with our budget and hopes it will be enough. The other begins with God and knows he will provide enough. As Paul wrote to Timothy in another letter, we can always trust the one "who richly gives us all we need for our enjoyment" (1 Timothy 6:17).

How I praise the Lord that you are concerned about me again. I know you have always been concerned for me, but you didn't have the chance to help me.

4:10

Not every church gave Paul gifts. In fact, Paul seems to have resisted any support from churches while he was ministering to them, primarily to avoid any appearance of preaching for financial gain (see 2 Corinthians 11:7-9; 2 Thessalonians 3:8-9). But the Philippians had given to Paul's ministry early on, and after a lapse in their giving—Paul isn't clear on why or how long, only that they were now concerned again—they renewed their support. Perhaps they recognized his predicament as a prisoner in Rome, having to pay for his own food and lodging but with no means to earn income. Maybe they would have helped earlier but couldn't—Paul had told the Corinthians that the Macedonian churches (for example, the one in Philippi) were "very poor" (2 Corinthians 8:1-2)—but now were more capable or more inclined to make sacrifices for the cause. In any case, Paul praised God for this new commitment and saw their giving as exceptional among the churches he had served (Philippians 4:15). Above all, the heart behind the gift was a cause for joy.

In Paul's mind, this act of giving, along with their common mission, made the Philippian believers "partners" in ministry (1:5). Though Paul's ministry was unique, he made no assumption that he was *the* minister while other believers were merely the supporters. He would have decried the model of church leadership that demarcates pastors and teachers as the only ministers and those in the congregation as something else, as if the body of believers equips its leaders rather than the leaders equipping the body for ministry. From Paul's perspective, the Philippians were merely carrying on what he and his ministry companions had started in Philippi, while he went around starting similar works in other cities. Together, they were spreading the good news of the Kingdom and building Kingdom communities. They were all in it together.

RE-ENVISION COMMUNITY

Practice seeing other believers in a new light. You are not just friends, fellow believers, colleagues, or co-workers. You are participants in the gospel. You probably don't have the same relationship with others that the apostle and this church had, but Paul's relationships with his churches have broader implications. Christians—fellow citizens of heaven—are in community together not only for fellowship but also for establishing the Kingdom culture here on earth. That includes sharing the gospel, to be sure, but it's more comprehensive. As Paul has made amply clear, a Kingdom culture involves radical transformation both inwardly and outwardly, in relationships not only between believers but also with others. Together we shine as lights in a dark world. This is a cooperative enterprise, a collective demonstration of the nature of God and the truth of his Word. Or, as Paul put it in the introduction to this letter, a partnership.

There's also another way to envision this relationship. The Kingdom is a family. It's a community joined together in familial bonds, with all the kinship, commitment, loyalty, sacrifice, togetherness—and sometimes dysfunction—those bonds imply. We are not just sharing good news; we are building up the family name and influencing the world with our unique characteristics. And as the Philippians did for Paul, we show our concern and pour out our lives for each other.

THE GOD WHO GIVES

Not that I was ever in need, for I have learned how to be content with whatever I have. I know how to live on almost nothing or with everything. I have learned the secret of living in every situation, whether it is with a full stomach or empty, with plenty or little.

4:11-12

The complexity of gift-giving in the ancient world made for tricky messaging. A simple expression of gratitude might have been perceived as an acknowledgment of indebtedness, a future obligation, or acceptance of a certain status. An acknowledgment of need might have triggered thoughts of clients and patrons, of benefactors and beneficiaries, or even of a further request for needs to be met. Paul certainly did not envision this gift within the confines of Greek and Roman giving protocols, but some of the Philippians might have. So his words of appreciation opened a door for him to reorient their vision, just in case. In the Kingdom, acts of generosity are not statements of status or obligation but statements of the heart. They are not a transaction. They represent a relationship of mutual support.

Paul avoids a misunderstanding by distancing his receipt of the Philippians' gift from any statement of need or dependence, though his needs are legitimate and substantial. In doing so, he makes profound statements about a believer's reasons for contentment, regardless of circumstances. He had learned the "secret" of shifting his focus from the means and amount of provision—*How will God provide? What should I do to support myself? Where is money going to come from? Will I have enough for my needs?*—to the bigger picture of his place in God's plans. A singular focus on pursuing Jesus will do that. It rivets our attention on our purpose and assumes that God will provide whatever is necessary for us to fulfill it.

Many Christians focus on Paul's statement that he had learned to get by with little. Few give much attention to his parallel statement that he had learned how to manage a lot. Paul knew God as a generous, abundant giver. He would not have seen poverty as a spiritual virtue; perhaps he saw it as only an occasional necessity. But his much greater focus was on how God provides in all seasons, one way or another, to one degree or another, and always enough. He was fixated only on the mission, not on the balance sheet, as important as that may be.

RE-ENVISION GOD'S PROVISION

Jesus told a parable of a master who gave his servants different amounts of money according to their abilities to manage it (Matthew 25:14-30). Two invested wisely and earned an increase. One buried his portion so he wouldn't lose any and could return the amount he was given. The risk-takers were commended; the hoarder was rebuked. The difference was in how they saw their master. Two recognized his goals; the other saw him as a "harsh man," a master who might not be very generous in a pinch.

Do you see God as someone who's reluctant to give? Do you feel like you have to pray the right prayers and jump through the right hoops to get his provision? Or can you relax in his generosity, knowing he'll give you whatever is needed (and often much, much more) in every season? Your vision of God has enormous implications for how you live, pray, and invest your life in his purposes. Paul had learned the secret of contentment. He rested in the certain knowledge of God's care. You can too.

IN ALL THINGS

I can do everything through Christ, who gives me strength.

4:13

In context, Paul is referring specifically to his ability to be content in all circumstances. Jesus gave him the strength to manage his circumstances and the vision to see beyond them, as Paul has exemplified so often in this letter. Whatever was going on in his life, Paul could deal with it because his focus was on pursuing Jesus and recognizing what God was doing through the circumstances around him. He had trained his mind to be content—an exercise in keeping with the principles of 4:8—and recognized what was most important. The spread of the gospel and the growth of the Kingdom constituted the big picture; everything else was details. With that focus, Paul could handle anything that came his way, including wide pendulum swings in the amount of support he had.

Yet Paul clearly was not referring *only* to contentment here. He wrote *everything*. We can safely assume he did not mean that Christ strengthened him for this matter alone. In fact, he relied on God's power in a wide range of situations. So he told the Corinthians that he focused only on the crucified Christ in his preaching so they would believe not in human persuasion but in God's power (1 Corinthians 2:1-5), and that God's power was made manifest in Paul's weakness (2 Corinthians 12:8-10), whatever form that weakness took.

He demonstrated a Spirit-dependent life both throughout his ministry as recorded in Acts and in his letters to the nascent churches.

So Paul broadened his statement from this context of contentment amid varying circumstances to point to the greater implications of Christ's empowerment. He certainly was not claiming some sort of magic wand, but neither would he ever say something as deprecating as "I'm only human." He was supernaturally enabled to be like Jesus, think like Jesus, and live like Jesus. He was more than a citizen of Rome or a citizen of earth. He was a citizen of heaven with access to heaven's provision and power. And, as with everything else in this letter, he was not making an exclusive claim. He was demonstrating an attitude and perspective for the Philippians (and us) to follow.

RE-ENVISION YOUR CAPABILITIES

As he did with Paul, Jesus will empower you to do anything you're called to do, whether it involves a mundane task, a thoroughly new attitude, or a Kingdom-promoting work. There's no reason to limit your expectations to whatever seems humanly possible, as minds rooted only in the here and now are so prone to do. Never claim that you're "only human," unless you mean that you are human in the sense of reflecting the divine image, being dependent on the Father, and being filled with the strength of his Spirit. Envision yourself as supernaturally empowered, as a citizen of heaven ought to be.

Whatever specific vision God gives you, whatever mission you've been called to accomplish, whatever purpose he has ordained for your life, whatever relationships you might need to restore, whatever attitudes you need to adopt as a follower of Jesus, whatever radical reorientation you might need to embrace in order to participate in and advance the culture of the Kingdom on earth, it's all available to you through the presence and power of Jesus. The Lord is near, working for you, in you, and through you in "everything."

KINGDOM INVESTMENTS

You Philippians were the only ones who gave me financial help when I first brought you the Good News and then traveled on from Macedonia. No other church did this. Even when I was in Thessalonica you sent help more than once.

4:15-16

The Philippians had a history of generosity. It wasn't because they were wealthy, as Paul made clear elsewhere (2 Corinthians 8:1-3). They gave because they wanted to, and apparently because they knew they could. They trusted God would provide for them, just as he provided for others through them. They acted like channels of Kingdom finances rather than people on a tight budget. They gave from the heart.

Hearts and treasures are inextricably linked in both directions. Jesus said as much when he spoke of investing our treasures in heaven (Matthew 6:19-21). We put money into the things we care about, and we care about what our money is invested in. For citizens of heaven, this ought to include heavy investments in eternal work—the mission of the Kingdom on earth. These are investments that earn everlasting interest. The increase of the Kingdom and its fruitfulness never end (see Isaiah 9:7). Wisdom directs our hearts and our wallets toward that ultimate purpose.

But in order to do that, we need more than a vision of eternity and how we can invest in it. No matter how committed we are to the never-ending growth of the Kingdom, we still have bills today. God is not just interested in meeting our barest needs while leaving anything above that to our own devices. There may be seasons of relative lack, and we should never turn the gospel into a mere health-and-wealth proposition, but God generally wants his people to thrive in every way—spiritually, emotionally, relationally, physically, and yes, often materially. He wants to be known as the God who provides, not just the God who helps us survive.

RE-ENVISION YOUR FINANCES

Adopting a lifestyle of Kingdom generosity requires two major shifts in the way we think. One is seeing our giving as an investment rather than as charity. Both are sacrifices, but charitable giving is a donation that may or may not involve us any further. Investing integrates us into the work as partners and provides benefits beyond simply knowing we helped. Paul has made clear that the Philippians were partners with him in the gospel. They gave as investors in the eternal work.

The other shift moves us from a scarcity mentality to an abundance mentality. Are we primarily contributors who only have so much to give from a fixed amount? Or are we children who know that whatever we give—regardless of the specific amount—the Father is going to adjust our provision accordingly (see 2 Corinthians 9:6-11)? People with a scarcity mentality give as though they are simply on a tight budget and must assume a limited supply. People with an abundance mentality give from the storehouses of heaven, knowing those storehouses never run dry. They assume God will always provide, even if they were to give away everything. The Kingdom is built on such trust. The sacrifices of a generous heart are rewarded in one form or another with the blessings of a generous God.

I don't say this because I want a gift from you. Rather, I want you to receive a reward for your kindness.

4:17

In some cultures, complimenting someone for an item they own is tantamount to saying you want it. They may even offer to give it to you, even if your intention was merely small talk. In ancient Greek and Roman cultures, stating a need or pointing out someone's generosity was often tantamount to asking for more—a statement Paul surely did not want to make. He was not mentioning the Philippians' history of giving (or its unexplained lapse) as a subtle hint for them to keep it up. So he redirected his words away from the benefit he received (which he did in fact need; see 4:14) to the benefit they would receive. He wanted them to be rewarded for their kindness.

Christians often shy away from the idea of rewards, but Scripture doesn't. Jesus mentioned them often (for example, Matthew 6:4; 10:41-42; 19:21, 29; Luke 6:38; 14:12-14); Paul referred to them too (for example, 1 Corinthians 3:12-15; Colossians 3:23-24)—even in this letter, he has mentioned the heavenly prize (Philippians 3:14)—and the idea of reward also appears often in the Old Testament and in Revelation. We don't want to be driven by rewards, as though we are serving only ourselves. But we also don't want to be unaware of them. The promise of rewards in this age and in the age to come is a compelling incentive. We need to understand that when we give our time, talents, or treasure, we are benefiting ourselves as well as others.

RE-ENVISION YOUR RESOURCES

If you think about it, all of life is an exercise in investments. At any given moment, you are giving and receiving, whether you want to be or not. You are pouring yourself into some idea, activity, or person, with thoughts, words, or behaviors that may be of little to no consequence or of enormous importance. But you're investing your time and attention somewhere. If your mind is wandering (not necessarily a bad thing), you are not problem-solving or praying or disciplining your thoughts. If you are preoccupied with one thing, you are neglecting another. If you are doing your job, you are investing in that work and receiving resources from it. Every moment is a choice, whether intentional or by default. We are always devoting ourselves to something.

When you see your life as a constant inflow and outflow of time, talent, treasure, ideas, relationships, and anything else that becomes the currency of your existence, you become more intentional about what's coming in and going out. Scripture in general, and Paul in this section of Philippians in particular, implicitly invites us to think about such things. Paul has already asked his readers to be stewards of joy, honorable and pure thoughts, prayer, finances, the privileges and perspectives of heavenly citizenship, and much more. We are stewards of these things too. When we receive from God and direct our entire lives in relation to his Kingdom, we thrive. We step out of the world's futility—its astonishing waste of God-given blessings—and into the abundant life Jesus promised. We bless and are blessed, pouring out and taking in, giving and receiving. And with those blessings come extravagant rewards.

POSITIVITY BIAS

At the moment I have all I need—and more! I am generously supplied with the gifts you sent me with Epaphroditus. They are a sweet-smelling sacrifice that is acceptable and pleasing to God.

4:18

It's human nature to focus on lack. We scan the horizons of our lives and notice what's missing, what's wrong, what needs to be fixed, or even what might need to be fixed one day. There's a name for this focus: negativity bias. It's what causes us to obsess about one critical comment rather than the hundreds of affirmations we've received, focus on the C on a child's report card rather than the six As surrounding it, or assume bad intentions when someone might have very good reasons for not responding yet. Many of us are visionaries of the glass half empty. Or even the glass 2 percent empty.

If Paul had any negativity bias in his past, it was gone by the time he wrote Philippians. Otherwise he would have been eaten up by the prospect of self-centered preachers, the injustice of accusations against him, the possibility of being executed, or the dilemma of paying for his own imprisonment. Instead he was filled with joy, hope, gratitude, contentment, and a peace that passes understanding. Never mind where his next provision might come from. His present provision, through the Philippians' gift, was more than enough. He had plenty—relatively speaking. He was taken care of—for now. They had renewed their concern for him—after a lapse. He refused to be consumed with gaps and lack and an uncertain future. He understood that whatever we focus on, whether good or bad, grows bigger in our minds. He was entirely focused on the good.

RE-ENVISION YOUR SITUATION

This is essentially Paul's instruction in 4:8—to dwell on the good. Well-meaning Christians often blast "positive thinking" as shallow and worldly, apparently never realizing how often and adamantly Scripture tells us to fill our minds with positive things. They mean to criticize efforts aimed at convincing ourselves of positive things that aren't true, but what about things that are? The Good News is indeed good, faith and hope are expectations of good, and God is working all things together for the good of those who love him (Romans 8:28). Human history ends remarkably well for those who believe. Refusing to have hope and joy in light of these realities is a denial of Scripture and God's promises. It's an affront to the Creator who called his work "very good" (Genesis 1:31) and still does. And it blatantly contradicts Paul's attitude throughout this letter.

Recognize whatever biases you may have, and if they need to be changed, be vigilant about turning them toward the truth, which is invariably good for those who trust God. Positive thinking based on fantasy is pointless, but positive thinking based on God's good promises and the hope he has commanded us to have is vital. Perhaps you, like Paul, have all you need at the moment, even if you aren't sure you will tomorrow. But Jesus said not to worry about tomorrow (Matthew 6:34). God cares for you and sustains you. In one way or another, you have been and will continue to be "generously supplied."

THE FAMILY BUSINESS

This same God who takes care of me will supply all your needs from his glorious riches, which have been given to us in Christ Jesus.

4:19

If you're a child whose mom or dad owns the family business, you have your run of the place. Employees need to follow certain protocols, but you have a different relationship with the owner. You aren't there to earn a paycheck, you don't have to produce anything, and you don't fit into any organizational chart. You're family. You enjoy whatever your parents accomplish simply because you're their child.

That's not an exact picture of our place in the Kingdom, but it's not too far off. Our Dad owns everything. It's already in his hands. Sure, there are some bad stewards out there who think they own what they have, but our Father has the whole world in his hands and is already intensely involved with everyone in it. When we pray, we're not asking him to step into a realm that isn't already his. We're asking him to do something in the family business he already operates. And when we give, we aren't losing precious resources. We're giving out of the endless abundance he already has.

Paul had very little at this point in his life. If he were operating within typical Greco-Roman giving protocols—which he has already clarified that he was not as he redirected the Philippians to Kingdom protocols instead—he would be obligated to respond to the Philippians' gift with assurances that he would take care of their needs. Having to support himself while in confinement, he was unable to do that, and the Philippians would not have expected him to. Nevertheless, he could offer something better. Their Father, who had always taken care of Paul's needs, would take care of these believers' needs too. And he would do so out of his glorious riches. These citizens of heaven could count on heaven's resources to compensate for their sacrificial giving.

RE-ENVISION THE FATHER'S BUSINESS

When we envision a world of limited resources and our Father operating outside of them, we pray for his intervention as though he is coming into a situation he otherwise would not. But when we envision the Kingdom of God as the family business and the entire universe as its holdings, any request for him to intervene is simply a matter of inviting him to do something that already falls under his domain. We may pray the same prayers either way, but with a different energy and perspective behind them. As with Paul, there is nothing frantic or anxious in our outlook. God already has it all. It's just a matter of distribution.

Never forget that you are a child of the God of glorious riches of all kinds. You have no need to pray, work, or live as an outsider. You have your run of the place, and you can ask him for whatever you want, as long as it fits the family culture and the business plans. You'll need discernment and patience as you ask, but all Kingdom attitudes, perspectives, resources, relationships, purposes, rights, and privileges are yours. You simply need to see who you are and have the faith and wisdom to receive and steward them well.

OUR FAMILY TIES

Give my greetings to each of God's holy people—all who belong to Christ Jesus. . . . All the rest of God's people send you greetings, too, especially those in Caesar's household. May the grace of the Lord Jesus Christ be with your spirit.

4:21-23

Paul ends this letter with further greetings—again to all God's "holy people" (4:21; see also 1:1), his label for everyone who has believed, no matter where they are in their journey toward maturity in Christ. Paul's world was once made up of two kinds of people: Jews and Gentiles. It is still made up of two kinds of people, but now classified along different lines: those who belong to Christ and those who don't (yet). Those who do belong are family. The "brothers" who were with him in Rome (4:21), including some among "Caesar's household" (4:22), send their greetings too. Even at a distance, this is one united fellowship.

At this point in Christian history, believers were scattered throughout the Mediterranean world (and perhaps a little beyond) in small, minority communities in diverse cities. Just as diaspora Jews shared a common bond—a loose one in some places, tighter in others—so did Christians. In other letters, Paul casts a vision of one body united not only in common beliefs but in one Spirit (for example, Ephesians 2:16-18; 4:3-6). The head of this body is Christ, and its members are filled with his Spirit and living out his resurrection life on earth. Separated by tens, hundreds, even thousands of miles, they were literally one spiritual family.

RE-ENVISION YOUR SPIRITUAL FAMILY

This familial bond is still our reality, of course, even if many Christians don't see themselves as very united with other branches of our faith. In one final example in this letter of the new vision we've been given, Paul assumes that "God's holy people" are tied together—certainly in bonds of friendship, but also in this new identity as those set apart for God's purposes. From God's perspective, this unity is real whether his people acknowledge it or not (John 17:20-23). The New Testament as a whole treats this new community as a living organism enlivened and empowered by Jesus himself, no matter how much distance stands between its members.

Many Christians in the past have considered themselves not just fellow believers (which we are) but also brothers and sisters in Christ, and many still do today. Embrace that vision and cultivate it wherever and however you can. In spite of whatever differences we have, everyone born of God's Spirit is family. That's a bond that cannot be broken, and it's a bond we are called to honor now and forever.

CONCLUSION

Looking back over the letter, we can see a lot of big-picture thoughts for people who may have been thinking small. Paul casts the story of God's Kingdom (and its King) over the smaller stories of his and the Philippians' circumstances, hoping to pull his readers out of their limited vision. Along the way, he has provided numerous case studies from his own experiences in adopting the worldview of the Kingdom. Paul has

- refused to feel defeated, worried, or anything less than joyful;
- refused to be distracted from his singular pursuit of knowing Jesus;
- made a case for both truth and love, but always leading with love, not the other way around;
- reoriented this fellowship's earthbound perspective to something much more transcendent; and
- insisted that God has been, is currently, and always will be working out his purposes through those who have entered into a relationship with him.

For anyone who has ever struggled with a troubling thought life, Philippians is a wonderful tool for retraining by immersion. When we saturate ourselves in its outlook, our hearts and minds change.

In a sense, the letter's overarching theme is becoming like Jesus (and becoming like Paul, who is becoming like Jesus). In doing so, we are to live as Kingdom citizens, establish Kingdom communities filled with the atmosphere of heaven, and pursue Kingdom purposes—including intimate knowledge of the King himself through participation in his incarnation, humility, sacrifice, and exaltation. Almost every takeaway from this letter relates to the template we've been given in Christ, including how to live out the notion that ultimately, he reigns over everything—and has given us the privilege of being stewards of his Kingdom on earth.

This is an enormous, life-shaping vision. As participants in the life of Jesus, we learn to see ourselves as carriers of his Kingdom, bringing hope, joy, love, and life. When people around us are bitter, depressed, or resistant, the temptation is to react in a similar way. But as we learn to see ourselves as Kingdom carriers, bearing a message and lifestyle that is truly good, we won't. We'll bring the opposite spirit of whatever doesn't look like the Kingdom, and sooner or later, if we persist, it will change the environment. Just as the Philippian believers were instructed, we will shine as lights in a dark world.

Like Paul, we can speak life into the people and situations around us. That may sometimes involve tearing down whatever quenches life—Paul certainly did that at times—but mostly it involves building up. We must learn to assess our fruitfulness by the questions of Kingdom citizenship:

How have I poured life into others?

Am I experiencing the atmosphere of heaven within me and reproducing it around me?

Am I leading with love and following with truth or reversing the order and sending the wrong message?

Do I end each day knowing the Kingdom has come a little further and grown a little stronger than when the day began?

How you answer these questions largely determines how you spend your days and how your vision shapes your life.

Remember that you are not a victim of circumstances. Paul makes that clear throughout this letter. You are a vessel of Kingdom life who spreads love, truth, joy, grace, peace, beauty, and purpose into every situation. If that's how you come to see yourself, everything else in your life, even adversity, becomes a platform for revealing the attributes of God. If you are going to live as a demonstration of the Kingdom in the world, highlighting the character of the Kingdom, it has to be within the circumstances you're facing. Otherwise it isn't a very clear demonstration.

For example, if you're going to demonstrate grace, it will have to be in the presence of people who need grace. If you're going to bring healing, it will have to be in the presence of people who need healing. If you're going to be a reconciler, it will have to be in the context of broken relationships and discord. These are necessary conditions for displaying God's Kingdom in your life and in the world.

That perspective sheds a whole new light on your circumstances, doesn't it? Instead of circumstances victimizing or oppressing you, they become vehicles for expressing who God is and what he is like—how the ways of his Kingdom are different from the ways of the world. Paul demonstrates this perspective at various points throughout this letter, and his demonstration is our invitation. If you envision every area of your life as an occasion to display something of the Kingdom of God in your responses and interactions, everything becomes a cause for rejoicing.

Above all, prioritize joy. Let joy become the climate of your heart—and of your relationships with others. There's a reason Paul emphasized joy again and again in this letter. It fills the environment of heaven and is therefore one of the key attributes of heaven's people. It brings heaven to earth as powerfully as any attitude can. As we put it at the forefront of our vision, it will change the way we think and live. There's no better way to shine in this world.

Acknowledgments

Tracing one's own knowledge to its original sources can be a nearly impossible task. I'm extremely grateful to have benefited from numerous sermons, lectures, commentaries, articles, essays, study materials, and personal conversations over the years, yet I can hardly remember any of them specifically. Our minds often work that way; they assimilate the information we receive and internalize it as "general understanding," as if we came into it ourselves, even when we know we didn't. So it is with my familiarity with Philippians. I owe a debt to many influences I wish I remembered well enough to thank.

But I can at least acknowledge those whose works I consulted in preparation for writing this devotional commentary, including Clinton Arnold, Stephen Fowl, Craig Keener, Ben Witherington, and Tim Woodroof. To these and many others, thank you for sharing your insights and expertise.

I am also grateful for the editorial team at Tyndale House Publishers, especially Jon Bryant for his careful and insightful work on this manuscript, as well as my agent, Mark Sweeney, for his encouragement and ever-reliable advice.

And, of course, I will forever be thankful for my wife, Hannah, and the rest of my family for their thoughtful questions, stimulating conversation, comic relief, enduring patience, and unwavering support.

May God fill the lives of all with blessing upon blessing.

Discussion Guide

This devotional commentary works well for individual use, but studying Scripture with other people and discussing biblical truths and insights is a great way to wrestle with and reinforce what you're learning. The following discussion prompts are organized into six manageable, thematic groupings to help get that conversation started. Feel free to condense these groupings into fewer sessions, divide them into more, or adapt them as you wish, depending on your needs and schedule. Do not feel compelled to discuss every question in every section. These are simply suggestions for touching on some of the most important themes of the book.

SESSION 1: BACKGROUND AND THEMES

1. Read Acts 16:11-40. On Paul's first visit to Philippi, long before he wrote his letter to the believers there, he and Silas expressed joy during very painful, difficult circumstances (see verse 25).

    a. Why do you think Paul and Silas were able to worship even though they had experienced the aches and pains from their beating, the uncomfortable chains that bound them, and the seeming hopelessness of their situation?

    b. What kind of testimony did their prayers and praises create for prisoners who were listening?

    c. In what ways did this experience foreshadow and demonstrate the themes of Philippians?

2. Imagine being a member of a small sect—less than 2 percent of your city's population—in a society that generally holds your "strange" beliefs in contempt.

    a. In what ways would you feel threatened by the culture around you? Try to make a positive impact in it? Feel the need to guard your reputation?

    b. Do you think you would feel discouraged and defeated by the opposition against you or encouraged by the hope and possibilities of your calling to reach people? Why?

3. It is often said that lifestyles and behavior are "more caught than taught."

    a. How have you observed this in your life or the lives of others?

    b. Why might early believers have needed both instruction and examples as they learned to live out their faith?

SESSION 2: PHILIPPIANS 1:1-26

1. Do you tend to view God through the lenses of your circumstances or view your circumstances through the lens of God? How does this shape your perceptions of your experiences? Of your understanding of other people? Of your sense of well-being?

2. What discrepancies are you aware of between the way you see yourself and the way God sees you? In what ways does your sense of identity shape your life?

3. What are some signs or symptoms of living in a "small picture"? What is different about living in the "big picture"? What steps can we take to make sure we live in a way that reflects what really matters?

4. Do you tend to see adversity and crisis situations as setbacks or opportunities? How would your perspective on life change if you saw every situation, good or bad, as an opportunity for God to work out his purposes for good?

5. In what ways did Paul see his situation as a stage for honoring Christ? Why did that make the prospect of death a secondary issue for him? What hinders us from rearranging our priorities similarly? How would your life change if you did?

SESSION 3: PHILIPPIANS 1:27–2:11

1. What practical implications does seeing yourself as a "citizen of heaven" have (see 1:27)? How might a vision of being seated with Christ in heavenly realms (Ephesians 2:6) change how you live? How would it affect your approach to adversity?

2. Why do you think Paul calls suffering for Christ a "privilege" (Philippians 1:29)? What does a positive perspective on adversity reveal about our faith? In what ways does it honor Jesus?

3. Do you tend to see members of the body of Christ as independent individuals or dependent parts of an organic whole? What difference does this make for our sense of fellowship?

4. In what ways does gazing at Jesus—being preoccupied with his nature—transform us?

5. What is the divine trajectory described by Paul in 2:6-11? How does this trajectory challenge our instincts? What do you think would happen if we lived out this paradigm in our relationships? Our work? Our major life decisions?

SESSION 4: PHILIPPIANS 2:12-30

1. Paul told the Philippians that God was shaping their desires and empowering them to carry out his purposes (2:13). How can we know which desires are ours and which are God's? How can we know when we are relying on his power and not our own?

2. What are the implications of being a child of God and living from that identity, as opposed to seeing ourselves only as a servant, believer, or follower?

3. Do you see yourself as a shining light in the world around you? Why or why not?

4. In what ways can Kingdom citizens express, demonstrate, and embody Kingdom character and values?

5. To what extent and in what ways do you think words are powerful? What does that tell us about our potential to shape lives with affirmation and honor?

SESSION 5: PHILIPPIANS 3:1–4:1

1. What does Paul mean by putting "no confidence in human effort" (3:3)? Does this mean we play no part in our own righteousness? Why or why not?

2. To what degree do the Christians you know live as though knowing Christ has "infinite value" (3:8)? To what degree do you? In practical terms, what does pursuing him above all else look like?

3. Paul emphasized putting the past behind him—not only his sins and regrets but also his rich cultural identity and heritage. Why is it important to find our primary identity and meaning so exclusively in Christ? In what areas do you need to identify with him more thoroughly?

4. To what degree and in what ways can believers, as citizens of heaven, create fellowship on earth that reflects our heavenly origins? What role do you think we play, individually and corporately, in revealing heaven's characteristics to the world around us? How do we become testimonies of hope for hurting people?

SESSION 6: PHILIPPIANS 4:2-23

1. In what respects do your thoughts influence the world? If our hearts and minds are incubators for faith, and if faith is powerful, to what degree should we guard and cultivate the thoughts, feelings, and attitudes within us?

2. In what sense is joy imperative? Why is Paul so insistent on it throughout this letter?

3. Why is worry so destructive? What kind of thoughts should we replace it with?

4. How is prayer an antidote to anxiety? In what ways does thankful prayer move our minds and hearts from an earthly environment toward a heavenly one?

5. Do you tend to see God as generous or sparing in his gifts and answers to prayers? How does this perspective of him shape our own level of generosity?

6. Do you currently feel powerless in any situation? If so, how does Paul's "secret" (4:12) relate to that sense of helplessness? More specifically, how does the promise of 4:13 address the gap between your natural ability and Jesus' supernatural ability? How can we access the strength of Christ in any situation?

About the Author

CHRIS TIEGREEN has touched the lives of millions of people through his twenty-seven books, forty-plus study and discussion guides, many magazine and newspaper articles, and joint projects with other communicators. He has authored nine One Year devotionals, and his curricular and collaborative works have been translated into more than sixty languages, reaching many countries around the world. His experience in media, ministry, and higher education brings a unique perspective to his writing, which ranges from biblical teaching and devotional themes to cultural and historical commentary. Chris and his wife live in Atlanta.

NOTES